THE HOLY SPIRIT

The Holy Spirit

Who He Is and What He Does

and

How to Know Him in All the Fulness of His Gracious and Glorious Ministry

By

R. A. TORREY, D.D.

Author of "Soul-Winning Sermons;" "The Person and Work of the Holy Spirit," etc.

Fleming H. Revell Company

PREFACE

THE chapters in this book are really addresses on the Holy Spirit that I have given in the various cities in which I have held meetings during the last twenty-five years. Of course, the addresses have grown and been modified as I have gone from city to city. They have been greatly blessed of God in bringing multitudes of believers into a larger Christian experience and life, in stirring up and equipping many for intelligent service and directly or indirectly, in the conversion, I presume, of a very goodly company in Japan, China, Australia, India, England, Scotland, Ireland, Germany, and in various states of the Union. After Mr. Moody had heard the addresses in the earlier form in which they were given, he insisted that I should give them in every place I visited, and the demand for their publication has increased as the years have gone by.

Nearly two years ago, I brought out a volume entitled *Soul-Winning Sermons,* containing all the sermons that I ordinarily preached in the night meetings wherever I conducted a series of meetings covering four weeks. I intended to bring out also a companion volume, containing the morning or afternoon addresses that I give to Christians in a four-weeks series, but these addresses are for the most part devoted to two lines of teaching—teaching concerning prayer and teaching concerning the Holy Spirit and His Work. When this latter book was well under way, it seemed wise to divide it into two volumes:

one devoted entirely to the subject of Prayer, and the other devoted entirely to the related subject of the Holy Spirit and His Work. The volume on Prayer, entitled *The Power of Prayer and the Prayer of Power,* came out almost simultaneously with the volume, *Soul-Winning Sermons.* Since then I have been so almost incessantly engaged, both winter and summer, in conducting evangelistic meetings and Bible conferences, and in writing other books for which the publishers could not wait, that I have been unable to bring out the volume on the Holy Spirit until now.

The substance of these addresses may be found in books of mine already published, and when people have asked me if they could not get the addresses in printed form I have replied: "You can find the substance of them in my book, *The Person and Work of the Holy Spirit,* or in my other book, *What the Bible Teaches.*" But many who have secured those books have said: "We want the addresses in the form that you give them in your meetings, with the illustrations that you use and the applications and personal appeals that you make." So here they are, and it is hoped that God may use them in the printed form even as He has so wonderfully used them when spoken from the platform.

In the present book there is no attempt to treat this great subject in a thorough and comprehensive way and in all its manifold bearings. If one desires to find such treatment of the subject he is referred to my book, *The Person and Work of the Holy Spirit,* in which it is attempted to give an exhaustive treatment of this important subject. The aim of this book is altogether practical; viz., to produce immediate results of definite personal blessing in the heart and life and service of every one who reads it.

Anyone who has this volume and the books, *Soul-Winning Sermons* and *The Power of Prayer and the Prayer of Power,* and my smaller book, *Getting the Gold Out of the Word of God,* has practically all the sermons and addresses that I give in any evangelistic campaign of ordinary length. However, not all the sermons that I preach in my longer series of meetings—covering, for example, three continuous months each (as in Liverpool and in Philadelphia), or covering five continuous months (as in London),—are in print, nor even in manuscript form.

R. A. T.

CONTENTS

CONTENTS

I

THE PERSONALITY OF THE HOLY SPIRIT

WE begin herewith a series of studies of the person and work of the Holy Spirit. We shall begin this series by considering what the Bible has to say about the Holy Spirit as a person. It is impossible to rightly understand the work of the Holy Spirit, or to get into right relation with the Holy Spirit Himself and thus know His blessed work in our own souls, without first coming to know the Holy Spirit as a person. One of the most fruitful sources of error and misconception, of unwholesome enthusiasm and false fire and fanaticism, in the treatment of this whole subject, is from trying to know the work of the Holy Spirit before we first come to know the Holy Spirit Himself. So my subject today is, " The Personality of the Holy Spirit."

To many of you doubtless that will seem like a rather abstract, abstruse, and impractical subject to take up with a popular audience. I do not blame you if you think so, for I can remember very distinctly the time when I so thought. I recall the first popular address that I ever heard upon the subject of the personality of the Holy Spirit. It was given by the late Dr. James H. Brooks, of St. Louis, that giant of Bible teaching. It was given in St. Paul, Minnesota. As I say, it was the first popular address that I had ever heard on that subject. Of course I had heard lectures upon the subject in the theological seminary, but this was an address before a popular audience.   When Dr. Brooks had finished his address I said to myself, "Well, Dr. Brooks has proved his point, the Holy Spirit certainly is a person; but what difference does it make anyhow whether the Holy Spirit is a Divine Person, or whether the Holy Spirit is a Divine Influence which God the Father, Who doubtless is a person, sends into our hearts? It is divine anyhow."

But I afterward came to find out that it made all the difference in the world. I discovered from the study of the Word of God, and from my own experience and the experience of others, that the doctrine of the personality of the Holy Spirit is not only fundamental, but vital and immeasurably practical.   Any one who does not know the Holy Spirit as a person has not attained unto a complete and well rounded Christian experience.   Any one who knows God the Father, and God the Son, and does not know God the Holy Spirit, has not attained unto the Christian conception of God, nor to a fully Christian experience.

I. The Importance of the Doctrine of the Personality of the Holy Spirit

1.   In the first place, *the doctrine of the personality of the Holy Spirit is of the highest importance from the standpoint of worship.* If the Holy Spirit is a person, and a Divine Person, and He is; and if you or I do not know Him as such, if we think of the Holy Spirit merely as an impersonal influence or power, as so many do, then we are robbing a Divine Person of the worship which is His due, of the love which is His due, and of the faith and confidence and surrender and obedience and worship which are His due.   May I stop just here to ask each one of you,

" Do you worship the Holy Spirit? " Theoretically we all do every time we sing the long metre Doxology:

> " Praise God from whom all blessings flow,
> Praise Him all creatures here below,
> Praise Him above, ye heavenly hosts,
> Praise Father, Son, *and Holy Ghost*."

Theoretically we all do every time we sing the Gloria Patri:

> " Glory be to the Father,
> And to the Son,
> And *to the Holy Ghost*.
> As it was in the beginning,
> Is now,
> And ever shall be,
> World without end. Amen."

But it is one thing to do a thing theoretically, and it is quite another thing to actually do it. It is one thing to sing words, it is quite another thing to realize the meaning and the force of the words that you sing.

I had a very striking illustration of this some years ago. I was going to a Bible Conference in New York State. I had to pass a city four miles from the grounds where the Conference was held. I had a relative living in that city and on the way to the Conference I stopped to call upon my relative, who went with me to the Conference. This relative was a Christian, she was much older than I, and had been a Christian much longer than I, and a member of the Presbyterian Church at that, brought up on the Shorter Catechism, and thoroughly Orthodox. I spoke that morning at the Conference on the Personality of the Holy Spirit. When the address was over and we were waiting on the veranda of the hotel for the trolley to take us back to the city, my relative turned to me and said, " Archie,

I never thought of *It* before as a person." Well, I had never thought of " *It* " as a person, but thank God I had come to know *Him* as a Person.

2. In the second place, *It is of the highest importance from a practical standpoint that we know the Holy Spirit as a Person.* If you think of the Holy Spirit, as so many even among Christian people do today, as a mere influence or power, then your thought will constantly be, " How can I get hold of the Holy Spirit and use it? " But if you think of Him in the Biblical way, as a Person of Divine majesty and glory, your thought will be, " How can the Holy Spirit get hold of me and use me? " Is there no difference between the thought of man, the worm, using God to thresh the mountain, or God using man, the worm, to thresh the mountain? The former conception, the conception of man using God to thresh the mountain, is heathenish; it does not differ essentially from the African fetish worshipper who uses his god. The latter conception, the thought of God the Holy Spirit getting hold of us and using us, is lofty, Christian, sublime.

Furthermore, if you think of the Holy Spirit merely as an influence or power that you are to get hold of and use, your thought will necessarily be, " How can I get more of the Holy Spirit? " But if you think of Him in the Biblical way, *as a Person,* your thought will be, " How can the Holy Spirit get more of me? "

The former conception, the conception of the Holy Spirit as a mere influence or power that you and I are to get hold of and use, leads inevitably to self-confidence, and self-exaltation, and a parade of self. If you think of the Holy Spirit as an influence or power that you are to get hold of and use, and then fancy that you have received the Holy Spirit, the inevitable result will be that you will strut around as if you belonged to a superior order of Christians. How much we see of that sort of thing. I remember a woman who once came to me at the Northfield Bible Conference at the close of an address and she said to me, "Brother Torrey, I want to ask you a question, but before I do, I want you to understand that *I am a Holy Ghost woman.*" My, it made me shudder, it sent a chill over me. It did not sound like it. But, on the other hand, if you think of the Holy Spirit in the Biblical way, as a Divine Person of infinite majesty, Who comes to dwell in our hearts and take possession of us and uses us as He wills, not as we will, it leads to self-renunciation, self-abnegation, self-humiliation. I know of no thought that is more calculated to put one in the dust and keep one in the dust, than this great Biblical truth of the Holy Spirit as a Divine Person coming to take up His dwelling in our hearts, and to take possession of our lives and to use us as He in His infinite wisdom sees fit.

3. In the third place, *The doctrine of the Personality of the Holy Spirit is of the highest importance from the standpoint of experience.* Thousands and tens of thousands of Christian men and women can testify to an entire transformation of their experience and of their service through coming to know the Holy Spirit as a Person. This address upon the Personality of the Holy Spirit which, for substance, I have given in almost every city in which I have ever held a series of meetings, is in some respects seemingly upon the most abstruse and technical subject that I ever attempt to handle before a popular audience, and yet, notwithstanding that fact, more men and women have come to me at the close of

this address, and more have written to me afterwards concerning it, testifying of personal blessing received, than of any other address which God has ever permitted me to give.

II. Four Lines of Proof of the Personality of the Holy Spirit

There are four separate and distinct lines of proof of the Personality of the Holy Spirit.

1. The first line of proof of the Personality of the Holy Spirit is that, *All the distinctive marks or characteristics of personality are ascribed to the Holy Spirit in the Bible.* What are the distinctive marks or characteristics of personality? Knowledge, feeling and will. Any being who knows and feels and wills is a person. Oftentimes when you say that the Holy Spirit is a Person, people understand you to mean that the Holy Spirit has hands, and feet, and fingers, and toes, and eyes, and ears, and nose, and mouth, and so on. No, not at all. These are not the marks of *personality;* these are the marks of *corporeity.* THE MARKS OF PERSONALITY ARE, KNOWLEDGE, FEELING AND WILL, AND ANY BEING WHO KNOWS, THINKS, FEELS, AND WILLS, IS A PERSON WHETHER HE HAVE A BODY OR NOT. You and I, if our earthly life ends before the Lord's return, will cease to have bodies for the time being; we will be "absent from the body, and at home with the Lord" (2 Cor. 5:8), but we shall not cease to be persons; we will be persons still, even though we have no body. I repeat it, the marks of personality are knowledge, feeling and will, and any being who knows and feels and wills is a person. Now all these marks, the marks of personality, are ascribed to the Holy Spirit in the Bible.

(1) Turn in your Bibles to 1 Cor. 2:11, "For what man knoweth the things of a man, save the spirit of man which is in him? even so the things of God knoweth no man, but the Spirit of God." *Here knowledge is ascribed to the Holy Spirit.* The Holy Spirit, in other words, is not a mere illumination that comes to your mind and mine, whereby our minds are enlightened and strengthened to see truth that they would not otherwise discover. No, the Holy Spirit is a Person who Himself knows the things of God and reveals to us what He Himself knows.

(2) Now turn to 1 Cor. 12:11 (R. V.): "But all these worketh the one and the same Spirit, dividing to each one severally *even as He will.*" The thought is that the Holy Spirit is not merely a Divine Power that we get hold of and use according to our will, but that the Holy Spirit is a Divine Person Who gets hold of us and uses us according to His will. This is one of the most fundamental truths in regard to the Holy Spirit, and we must ever bear it in mind if we are to come into right relations with Him and continue in right relations with Him. Countless earnest-minded Christians are going astray at this point. They are trying to get hold of some divine power which they can use according to their will. I thank God from the depth of my heart that there is no divine power that I can get hold of to use according to my will. What could I do in my foolishness and ignorance with a divine power? What evil I might work! But while I thank God that there is no divine power that I can get hold of and use in my foolishness and ignorance according to my will, I am still more glad that there is a Divine Person Who can get hold of me and use me according to His infinitely wise and loving will.

(3) Now turn to Romans 8 : 27, " And He that searcheth the hearts knoweth what is *the mind of the Spirit,*
because He maketh intercession for the saints according
to the will of God." What I wish you to note here is the
expression, " the *mind* of the Spirit." The Greek word
here translated " mind " is " phronema," and it is a comprehensive word that has in it all three ideas of knowledge, feeling and will. It is the same word which is used
in the seventh verse of this chapter, where we read, " The
mind of the flesh is enmity against God," where the
thought is that not merely the thought of the flesh is
enmity against God, but the whole moral and intellectual
life of the flesh is enmity against God.

(4) We now turn to a most remarkable passage,
Romans 15 : 30, " Now I beseech you, brethren, for the
Lord Jesus Christ's sake, and for *the love of the Spirit,*
that ye strive together with me in your prayers to God
for me." What I wish you to notice particularly in this
verse are these five words, " *The love of the Spirit.*" It
is a wonderful thought. It teaches that the Holy Spirit is
not a mere blind influence or power, no matter how
beneficent, that comes into our hearts and lives, but that
He Himself is a Divine Person, loving us with the ten-
derest love. I wonder how many of us have ever thought
much regarding " *the love of the Spirit* " ? I wonder how
many of us ministers who are here today have ever
preached a sermon on " The Love of the Spirit." I wonder how many of you have ever heard a sermon on " The
Love of the Spirit." I wonder how many of you have
ever thanked the Holy Spirit for His love. Every day
of your life you kneel down before God the Father, at
least I hope you do, and say, " Heavenly Father, I thank
Thee for Thy great love that led Thee to give Thy Son

Jesus Christ to come down into this sinful world and to die upon the cross of Calvary in my place." Every day of your life you kneel down and look up into the face of Jesus Christ the Son and say, " Thou blessed Son of God, I thank Thee for that great love of Thine that led Thee to come down to this world in obedience to the Father and to die in my place upon the cross of Calvary."

But do you ever kneel down and look up to the Holy Spirit and say to Him, " Holy Spirit, I thank Thee for Thy great love to me "? And yet we owe our salvation as truly to the love of the Spirit as we do to the love of the Father and the love of the Son. If it had not been for the love of God the Father to me, looking down upon me in my lost estate, yes, anticipating my fall and ruin and sending His own Son down to this world to die upon the cross in my place, I would have been a lost man today. If it had not been for the love of Jesus Christ the Son coming down to this world in obedience to the Father, and laying down His life, a perfect atoning sacrifice on the cross of Calvary in my behalf, I would have been a lost man today. But if it had not been for the love of the Holy Spirit to me, leading Him to come down to this world in obedience to the Father and the Son, to seek me out in my lost condition, following me day after day, and week after week, and month after month, and year after year, following me when I would not listen to Him, when I deliberately turned my back upon Him, when I insulted Him, following me into places where it must have been agony for that Holy One to go, following me day after day, week after week, month after month, year after year, until at last He succeeded in bringing me to my senses and bringing me to realize my utterly lost condition, and revealing the Lord Jesus to me as just the Saviour Whom

I needed and induced me and enabled me to receive the Lord Jesus as my Saviour and Lord; if it had not been for this patient, long-suffering, never-wearying love of the Spirit of God to me, I would have been a lost man today. If you get nothing else from this address today, let these words sink into your mind and heart, " THE LOVE OF THE SPIRIT."

(5) Turn now to a passage in the Old Testament, Neh. 9: 20, " Thou gavest also thy good Spirit to *instruct them,* and withheldest not thy manna from their mouth, and gavest them water for their thirst." *Here both intelligence and goodness are ascribed to the Holy Spirit.* This passage does not add anything to the thoughts that we have already had; I have brought it in merely because it is from the Old Testament. There are those who say that the doctrine of the Personality of the Holy Spirit is in the New Testament but not in the Old Testament; but here we find it as clearly in the Old Testament as in the New. Of course, we do not find it as frequently in the Old Testament as in the New, for this is the dispensation of the Holy Spirit, but the doctrine of the Personality of the Holy Spirit is there in the Old Testament.

There are many who say that the doctrine of the Trinity is not in the Old Testament, that while it is in the New Testament it is not in the Old Testament. But the doctrine of the Trinity is in the Old Testament in the very first chapter of the Bible. In Genesis 1: 26 we read, " And God said, *Let us* make man in Our image, after *Our likeness."* Here the plurality of the persons in the Godhead stands out clearly. God did not say, " I will," or, " Let *me* " " make man in my own image." No, He said, " Let *us* make man in *Our* image, after *Our likeness."* The three persons in the Trinity are found in the first three verses in the Bible, " In the beginning God created the heaven and the earth;" here we have God the Father. "And the earth was without form, and void, and darkness was upon the face of the deep. And *the Spirit* of God moved upon the face of the waters;" there you have the Holy Spirit. "And God said," there you have the Word, " Let there be light: and there was light." Here we have the three persons of the Trinity in the first three verses of the Bible.

In actual fact the doctrine of the Trinity is found many hundreds of times in the Old Testament. In the Hebrew Bible it occurs in most of the places where you find the word " God " in your English Bible, for the Hebrew word ordinarily used for God in the Old Testament is a plural noun; literally translated it would be " Gods," and not " God." In the very passage to which the Unitarians and Jews, who reject the Deity of Christ, refer so often as proving conclusively that the Deity of Christ cannot be true, namely, Deut. 6:4, the very doctrine that they are seeking to disprove is found; for Deut. 6:4, literally translated, would read, " Hear, O Israel: Jehovah our Gods is one Jehovah."

Why did the Hebrews, with their unquestionable and intense monotheism, use a plural name for God? This was the question that puzzled the Hebrew grammarians and lexicographers of the past, and the best explanation that they could arrive at was that the plural for God here used was " the pluralis majestatis," that is, the plural of majesty. But this explanation is entirely inadequate. To say nothing of the fact that the pluralis majestatis in the Old Testament is a figure of very doubtful occurrence— I have not been able to find any place in the Old Testament where it is clear that the pluralis majestatis is used—

but in addition to that, even if it were true that the pluralis majestatis does occur in the Old Testament, there is another explanation for the use of a plural name for God that is far nearer at hand and far more adequate and satisfactory, and that is, that the Hebrew inspired writers used a plural name for God, in spite of their intense monotheism, *because there is a plurality of persons in the one Godhead.*

(6) Now turn to Eph. 4:30, "And *grieve not* the Holy Spirit of God, whereby ye are sealed unto the day of redemption." *Here grief is ascribed to the Holy Spirit.* In other words, the Holy Spirit is not a mere blind, impersonal influence or power that comes to dwell in your heart and mine. No, He is a Person, a Person Who loves us, a Person Who is holy and intensely sensitive against sin, a Person Who recoils from sin in what we would call its slightest forms as the holiest woman on earth never recoiled from sin in its grossest and most repulsive forms. And He sees whatever we do, He hears whatever we say, He sees our every thought, not a vagrant fancy is allowed a moment's lodgment in our mind but what He sees it; and if there is anything impure, unholy, immodest, uncharitable, untrue, false, censorious, bitter, or unChristlike in any way, in word or thought or act, He is grieved beyond expression. This is a wonderful thought, and it is to me the mightiest incentive that I know to a careful walk, a walk that will please this indwelling Holy One in every act and word and thought.

How many a young man is kept back from doing things that He would otherwise do, by the thought that if he did do that his mother might hear of it and she would be grieved beyond expression. How many a young man who went over to France in the late war, and was surrounded by the awful temptations that encompassed our young men on every hand at that time and at that place, in some hour of fierce temptation stood at the door of a house that no self-respecting man ought ever to enter, and just as his hand was on the door-knob and he was about to open the door, the thought came to him, "If I should enter there mother might hear of it, and if she did it would nearly kill her," and he has turned away without entering. But listen, there is One holier than the holiest mother that you or I ever knew, One Who loves us with a more tender love than our own mother loves us, and He sees everything we do, not only in the daylight but under the cover of the night; He hears every word we utter, every careless word that escapes our lips; He sees every thought we entertain, yes, every fleeting fancy that we allow a moment's lodgment in our mind, and if there is anything unholy, impure, immodest, uncharitable, indecorous, unkind, harsh, bitter, censorious, or unChristlike in any way, in act or word or thought, He sees it and is grieved beyond expression. Oh, how often there has come into my mind some thought or imagination, from what source I do not know, but it is a thought I ought not to entertain, and just as I was about to give it lodgment the thought has come, "The Holy Spirit sees that and will be grieved by it," and the thought has gone.

Bearing this thought of the Holy Spirit in our mind will help us to solve all the questions that perplex the young believer in our day. For example, the question, "Ought I as a Christian to go to the theatre or the movies?" Well, if you go the Holy Spirit will go, too, for He dwells in the heart of every believer and goes wherever the believer goes. Were you ever in a theatre or moving picture show in your life where you honestly thought the atmosphere of the place would be congenial to the *Holy* Spirit? If not, do not go. Ought I as a Christian go to dances? Well, here again, if you go the Holy Spirit will surely go. Were you ever at a dance in all your life where you really believed the atmosphere of the place would be congenial to the *Holy* Spirit? Shall I as a Christian play cards? Were you ever at a card party in your life, even the most select little neighbourhood gathering, or even at a home gathering to play cards, where you thought the atmosphere of the place would be congenial to the *Holy* Spirit? If not, do not play. So with all the questions that come up and that some of us find so hard to settle, this thought of the Holy Spirit will help you to settle them all, and to settle them right (if you really desire to settle them right and not merely to do the thing that pleases yourself, even though it may grieve the Holy Spirit).

2. The second line of proof of the Personality of the Holy Spirit is that, *Many actions are ascribed to the Holy Spirit that only a person can perform.* There are many illustrations of this in the Bible, but I will limit our consideration today to three instances.

(1) Turn to the second chapter of 1 Corinthians. In the tenth verse we read, " But unto us God revealed them through the Spirit: for the Spirit searcheth all things, yea, the deep things of God." Here the Holy Spirit is represented as searching the deep things of God. In other words, as we have already said under our previous heading, the Holy Spirit is not a mere illumination whereby our minds are illumined and made strong to apprehend truth that they would not otherwise discover, but the Holy Spirit is a Person Who Himself searches into the deep things of God and *reveals* to us the things

which He discovers.   Such words, of course, could only
be spoken of a person.

(2) Now turn to Romans 8:26, " And in like manner
the Spirit also helpeth our infirmity: for we know not
how to pray as we ought; but the Spirit Himself *maketh
intercession for us* with groanings which cannot be uttered." *Here the Holy Spirit is represented as doing
what only a person can do,* that is, *He is represented as
praying.* The Holy Spirit is not merely an influence that
comes upon us and impels us to pray, nor is He a mere
guidance to us in offering our prayers.   No, no; *He is
Himself a Person Who Himself prays.*

Every believer in Christ has two Divine Persons praying for him every day: first, the Son, our " Advocate with
the Father," Who " ever liveth to make intercession for
us " up yonder at the right hand of God in the glory
(1 John 2:1 and Heb. 7:25); second, the Holy Spirit
Who prays through us down here on earth.   Oh, what a
wonderful thought, that each and every believer in Christ
has two Divine Persons praying for him every day.
What a sense it gives us of our security—I do not believe
the Devil will ever get us.

When I started around the world in 1901, I sent out
five thousand letters to people whom I had learned knew
how to pray, asking them if they would pray for Mr.
Alexander and me every day as we went around the
world.   One of the hardest tasks I ever had in my life
was signing those letters, signing my name five thousand
times, but it paid, for soon letters came back by the thousands from these persons saying that they would pray for
us every day.   When Mr. Alexander and I reached Melbourne, Australia, ten thousand people had taken it up
and were praying for us every day, and when we reached

England no less than forty thousand people were praying for us every day. Who could not preach under such circumstances, and is it any wonder that the marvellous results followed that did follow? I wish they were all praying for me still; but, while I would be glad to have those forty thousand people praying for me every day, if I had to choose between having forty thousand of the godliest men and women on earth praying for me every day, or to have those two Persons, Christ the Son, our Advocate with the Father, and the Holy Spirit, our Comforter, praying for me every day, I would choose the two rather than the forty thousand.

(3) Now turn to two closely related passages. John 14: 26, " But the Comforter, even the Holy Spirit, whom the Father will send in My name, He shall teach you all things, and bring to your remembrance all that I have said unto you." *Here the Holy Spirit is represented as doing what only a person could do,* namely, *teaching.* We have the same thought in John 16: 12-14: " I have yet many things to say unto you, but ye cannot bear them now. Howbeit when He, the Spirit of Truth, is come, He shall guide you into all the truth: for He shall not speak from Himself; but what things soever He shall hear, these shall He speak: and He shall declare unto you the things that are to come. He shall glorify Me: for He shall take of mine, and shall declare it unto you." Here again the Holy Spirit is represented as a living, personal teacher. It is our privilege today to have the Holy Spirit, a living Person, as our teacher.

Every time we study our Bible it is possible for us to have this Divine Person, the Author of the Book, to interpret it to us, and to teach us its real and its innermost meaning. It is a precious thought. How many of us have often thought when we heard some great human teacher whom God has especially blessed to us, " Oh, if I could only hear that man every day, then I might make some progress in my Christian life." But listen, we can have a teacher more competent by far than the greatest human teacher that ever spoke on earth for our teacher every day, and that peerless teacher is the Holy Spirit.

3. The third line of proof of the Personality of the Holy Spirit is that, *An office is predicated of the Holy Spirit that could only be predicated of a Person.* Look, for example, at John 14: 16, 17. Here we read, " And I will pray the Father, and He shall give you another Comforter, that He may abide with you for ever; even the Spirit of truth; Whom the world cannot receive, because it seeth Him not, neither knoweth Him: but ye know Him; for He dwelleth with you, and shall be in you." Here the Holy Spirit is represented as *another Comforter* who is coming to take the place of our Lord Jesus. Up to this time our Lord Jesus had been the friend always at hand to help them in every emergency that arose. But now He was going, and their hearts were filled with consternation, and He tells them that while He is going *Another is coming* to take His place. Can you for a moment imagine our Lord Jesus saying this if the other who is coming to take His place were a mere impersonal influence or power?

Can you imagine our Lord Jesus saying what He says in John 16:7, " Nevertheless I tell you the truth; *It is expedient for you that I go away:* for if I go not away, the Comforter will not come unto you; but if I depart, I will send Him unto you," if that which was coming to take His place were not another Person but a mere influence or power? In that case, is it for a moment conceivable that our Lord could say that it was expedient for Him, a Divine Person, to go and a mere influence or power, no matter how divine, come to take His place? No! No! WHAT OUR LORD SAID WAS THAT HE, ONE DIVINE PERSON, WAS GOING, BUT THAT ANOTHER PERSON, JUST AS DIVINE AS HE, WAS COMING TO TAKE HIS PLACE.

This promise is to me one of the most precious promises in the whole Word of God for this present dispensation, the thought that during the absence of our Lord, until that glad day when He shall come back again, another Person just as Divine as He, just as loving and tender and strong to help, is by my side always, yes, dwells in my heart every moment to commune with me and to help me in every emergency that can possibly arise.

I take it for granted that you know that the Greek word translated " Comforter " in these verses means far more than Comforter. It means Comforter plus a great deal beside. The Greek word so translated is " Parakletos." This word is a compound word, compounded of the word " Para," which means " alongside," and " Kletos," which means " one called ": so the whole word means, " One called to stand alongside another," one called to take his part and help him in every emergency that arises.

It is the same word that is translated " Advocate " in 1 John 2:1, " If any man sin, we have an *Advocate* (Parakleton) with the Father, Jesus Christ the righteous." But the word " Advocate " does not begin to give the full force of the word. Etymologically the word " Advocate " means about the same as the word " Parakletos." Advocate is really a Latin word transliterated into the English; the word is compounded of two words,

" ad," meaning " to," and " vocatus," which means " one called;" that is to say, Advocate means one called to another to take his part, or to help him. But in our English usage this word Advocate has obtained a narrower and more restricted sense. The Greek word, as I have already said, means " One called alongside another," and the thought is of a helper always at hand with His counsel and His strength and any form of help that is needed.

Up to this time the Lord Jesus Himself had been their Paraclete, the friend always at hand to help. Whenever they got into any trouble they simply turned to Him. For example, on one occasion they were perplexed on the subject of prayer and they said to the Lord, " Lord, teach us to pray," and He taught them to pray. On another ocasion when Jesus was coming to them walking on the water, when their first fear was over and He had said, " It is I, be not afraid," then Peter said unto Him, " Lord, if it be Thou, bid me come unto Thee upon the water." And the Lord said, " Come." Then Peter clambered over the side of the fishing-smack and commenced to go to Jesus, walking on the water. He got along fine for a few moments, and then seemingly he turned around to see if his companions saw how well he was doing, thus he took his eyes off the Lord and saw the wind and the waves, and no sooner had he gotten his eyes off the Lord than he began to sink, and he cried out, " Lord, save me," and Jesus reached out His hand and held him up. Just so, when they got into any other emergency the disciples turned to the Lord and He delivered them. But now He was going and consternation filled their hearts, and the Lord said to comfort them, " Yes, I am going, but another just as Divine as I, just as loving and tender as I, just as able to help in every emergency that may arise, is coming to take my place," and this other Paraclete is with us wherever we go, every hour of the day or night. He is always at our side. Precious and wondrous thought!

If this thought gets into your heart and stays there, you will never have another moment of fear as long as you live. How can we fear under any circumstances if we really believe that He is by our side? You may be surrounded by a howling mob; I have been, an Irish mob and a Chinese mob, but what of it, if He walks between you and the mob? That thought will banish all fear. I had some years ago a striking illustration of this in my own experience that I shall never forget. I was speaking at a Bible Conference on a lake in New York State. I had a cousin who had a cottage four miles up the lake and I went up there and spent my rest day with him. The next day he brought me down in his steam launch to the pier where the Conference was held. As I stepped off the launch onto the pier he said to me, " Come back again tonight, Archie, and spend the night with us," and I promised him I would. But I did not realize what I was promising. That night, when my address was over, as I went out of the hotel and started on my walk, I found that I had taken a large contract. The cottage was four miles away, but a four-mile walk or an eight-mile walk was nothing to me under ordinary circumstances, but a storm was coming up and the whole heaven was overcast. Furthermore, the path led along a bluff bordering the lake, and the path was near the edge of the bluff. Sometimes the lake was perhaps not more than ten or twelve feet below, at other times some thirty or forty feet below. I had never gone over the path before and found that it led right along the edge of the bluff; besides that, there was no starlight and I could not see the path at all. There had already been a storm that had gulleyed out deep ditches across the path into which one might fall and break his leg. I could not see these ditches except when there would be a sudden flash of lightning, when I would see one, and then it would be darker and I blinder than ever.

As I walked along this path, so near the edge of the bluff with all the furrows cut through it, I felt it was perilous to take the walk and thought of going back; but the thought came to me, " You promised that you would come tonight and they may be sitting up waiting for you," so I felt that I must go on. But it seemed creepy and uncanny to walk along the edge of the bluff on such an uncertain path which I could not see, and could only hear rising from the foot of the bluff the sobbing and wailing and the moaning of the lake as it was moved by the fast approaching storm. Just then the thought came to me, " What was it you told the people there at the Conference about the Holy Spirit being a Person always by our side? Does He not walk by your side now?" Then I at once realized that the Holy Spirit walked between me and the edge of the bluff, and that four miles through the dark was four miles without fear, a gladsome instead of a fearsome walk.

I once threw this thought out in the Royal Albert Hall in London, one dark dismal afternoon. There was a young lady in the audience who had an abnormal fear of the dark. It simply seemed impossible for her to go into a dark room alone. After the meeting was over she hurried home and rushed into the room where her mother was sitting and cried, " Oh, mother, I have heard the most wonderful address this afternoon I ever heard in my life, about the Holy Spirit always being by our side as our ever-present helper and protector. Mother, I shall never be afraid of the dark again." But her mother was a practical English woman, and said to her, " Well, let us see how real that is. Now, go up-stairs to the top floor, into the dark room, and shut the door and stay in there alone in the dark." The daughter wrote me the next day, " I went bounding up the stairs, went into the dark room, closed the door and it was pitch dark, and Oh, it was dark, utterly dark, but that room was bright and glorious with the presence of the Holy Spirit."

In this thought of the Holy Spirit as a Person ever present with us, is also a cure for insomnia. Did any of you ever have insomnia? I did. For two dark, awful years. Night after night I would go to bed almost dead, it seemed to me, for sleep, and I thought I would certainly sleep as I could scarcely keep awake; but scarcely had my head touched the pillow when I knew I would not sleep, and I would hear the clock strike twelve, one, two, three, four, five, six, and then it was time to get up. It seemed as though I had not slept at all, though I have no doubt I did; for I believe that people who suffer from insomnia sleep far more than they think they do, else we would go insane or die, but it seemed as if I did not sleep at all. This went on for two long years, until I thought that if I could not get sleep I would lose my mind. And then I got deliverance. For years I would retire and fall asleep about as soon as my head touched the pillow. But one night I went to bed in the Bible Institute in Chicago, where I was then stopping. I expected to fall asleep almost immediately, as had become my custom, but scarcely had my head touched the pillow when I knew I was not going to sleep. Insomnia was back. If you have ever had him you will always recognize him. It seemed as if Insomnia was sitting on the footboard of my bed looking like an imp, grinning at me and saying, "I am back for two more years."

"Oh," I thought, "two more years of this awful insomnia." But that very morning I had been teaching to our students, in the lecture-room on the floor below, the Personality of the Holy Spirit, and the thought came to me almost immediately, "What was that you were telling the students down-stairs this morning about the Holy Spirit being a Person always with us?" And I said to myself, "Why don't you practice what you preach?" And I looked up and I said, "Oh, Thou blessed Spirit of God, Thou art here; if Thou hast anything to say to me I will listen." And He opened to me some of the sweet and precious things about Jesus Christ that are found in the Word of God, filling my soul with calm and peace and joy, and the next thing I knew I was asleep, and the next thing I knew it was tomorrow morning. And whenever Insomnia has come around since and sat on my footboard, I have done the same thing and it has never failed.

In this thought of the Holy Spirit being a Personal friend always at hand, is also *a cure for all loneliness*. If the thought of the Holy Spirit as an Ever-present Friend, always at hand, once enters your heart and stays there, you will never have another lonely moment as long as you live.

My life for the larger part of the last twenty-five years has been a lonely life. I have often been separated from my family for months at a time, sometimes I have not seen my wife for two or three months at a time, and for eighteen months I did not even once see any member of my family except my wife. One night I was walking the deck of a steamer in the South Seas between New Zealand and Tasmania. It was a stormy night. Most of the other passengers were below, seasick, and none of the officers or sailors could walk with me, for they had their hands full looking after the boat. Four of the five members of my family were on the other side of the globe, seventeen thousand miles away by the nearest route that I could get to them, and the one member of my family who was nearer was not with me that night. As I walked the deck all alone I got to thinking of my four children seventeen thousand miles away and was about to get lonesome, when the thought came to me of the Holy Spirit by my side, and that as I walked up and down the deck in the night and in the storm He took every step with me, and all my loneliness was gone.

I gave expression to this thought some years ago in the City of St. Paul, and at the close of the address a physician said to me, " I wish to thank you for that thought. I am often called at night to go out alone through darkness and storm far into the country, and I have been very lonely, but I will never be lonely again, for I will know that every step of the way the Holy Spirit is beside me in my doctor's gig."

In this same precious truth of the Holy Spirit as a Personal Friend always at hand there is a cure for a broken heart. Oh, how many broken-hearted people there are in the world today. Many of us have lost loved ones, but we need not have a moment's heartache if we only know " *the communion* of the Holy Ghost." There is perhaps here today some woman who a year ago, or it may be only a few months or a few weeks ago, or possibly a few days ago, had by her side a man whom she dearly loved, a man so strong and wise that she was freed

from all sense of responsibility and care, for all the burdens were upon him. How bright and happy were the
days of his companionship! But the dark day came
when that loved one was taken away, and how lonely
and empty and barren and full of burden and care life
is today. Listen, woman, there is One Who walks right
by your side today, Who is far wiser and stronger and
more loving and more able to guide and help than the
wisest and strongest and most loving husband that ever
lived; ready to bear all the burdens and responsibility of
life for you, yes, ready to do far more, ready to come in
and dwell in your heart and fill every nook and corner of
your empty and aching heart, and thus banish the loneliness and all the heartache forever.

I said this one afternoon in St. Andrew's Hall in Glasgow. At the close of the address, when I went out into
the reception-room, a lady who had hurried out to meet
me, approached. She wore a widow's bonnet, her face
bore the marks of deep sorrow, but now there was a happy
look in her face. She hurried to me and said, " Dr. Torrey, this is the first anniversary of my dear husband's
death (her husband was one of the most highly esteemed
Christians in Glasgow), and I came to St. Andrew's Hall
today saying to myself, ' Dr. Torrey will have something
to say that will help me.' Oh," she continued, " you have
said just the right word. I will never be lonesome again,
never have a heartache again. I will let the Holy
Spirit come in and fill every aching corner of my heart."
Eighteen months passed, I was back in Scotland again,
taking a short vacation on the Lochs of the Clyde, on the
private yacht of a friend. One day we stopped off a
point, a little boat put off the point and came alongside
the steam yacht. The first one who clambered up the

side of the yacht and over the rail and onto the deck was this widow. Seeing me standing on the deck she hurried across and took my hand in both of hers and with a radiant smile on her face she said, " Oh, Dr. Torrey, the thought you gave me in St. Andrew's Hall that afternoon stays with me still, and I have not had a lonely or sad hour from that day to this."

But it is in our Christian work that the thought comes to us with greatest power and helpfulness. Take my own experience: I became a minister of the gospel simply because I had to, or be forever lost. I do not mean that I am saved by preaching the gospel; I am saved simply on the ground of the atoning blood of Jesus Christ, and that alone; but my becoming a Christian and accepting Him as my Saviour turned upon my preaching the gospel. For several years I refused to come out as a Christian because I was unwilling to preach, and I felt that if I became a Christian I must preach. The night that I surrendered to God I did not say, " I will accept Christ," or " I will give up my sins;" I said, " I will preach."

But if there was ever a man who by natural temperament was utterly unfitted to preach, it was I. I was an abnormally bashful boy, and a stranger could scarcely speak to me without my blushing to the roots of my hair. When I went away from home visiting with other members of my family, I could not eat enough at the table, I was so frightened to be among strangers. Of all the tortures I endured at school there was none so great as that of reciting a piece. To stand on the platform and have the scholars looking at me, I could scarcely endure it; and even when my own father and mother at home asked me to recite the piece to them before I went to school, I simply could not recite it before my own father and mother. Think of a man like that going into the ministry. Even after I was a student in Yale College, when I would go home on a vacation and my mother would have callers and send for me to come in and meet them, I could not say a word. After they were gone my mother would say to me, " Archie, why didn't you say something to Mrs. S—— or Mrs. D——? " and I would say, " Why, mother, I did." And she would reply, " You did not utter a sound." I thought I did, but it would get no further than my throat and stick there. I was so bashful that I never even spoke in a church prayer-meeting until after I entered the theological seminary. Then I thought that if I were to be a preacher I must at least be able to speak in my own church prayer-meeting. I made up my mind that I would. I learned a piece by heart, I remember some of it to this day, but I think I forgot some of it when I got up to speak that night. As soon as the meeting was open I grasped the back of the settee in front of me and pulled myself up to my feet and held on to it lest I should fall. One Niagara went rushing up one side and another down the other, and I tremblingly repeated as much of my little piece as I could remember, and then dropped back into the seat. At the close of the meeting a dear old maiden lady, a lovely Christian woman, came to me and said, " Oh, Mr. Torrey, I want to thank you for what you said tonight. It did me so much good, you spoke with so much feeling." Feeling? The only feeling I had was that I was scared nearly to death. Think of a man like that going into the ministry.

My first years in the ministry were torture. I preached three times a day. I committed my sermons to memory, and then I stood up and twisted the top button of my coat until I had twisted the sermon out, and then when the third sermon was preached and finished I dropped back into the haircloth settee back of the pulpit with a great sense of relief that that was over for another week. But then the dreadful thought would at once take possession of me, "Well, you have got to begin tomorrow morning to get ready for next Sunday." Oh, what a torment life was. But a glad day came, a day when the thought which I am trying to teach you now took possession of me, namely, that when I stood up to preach, that, though people saw me, that there was Another whom they did not see, but Who stood by my side, and that all the responsibility was upon Him and all I had to do was to get just as far back out of sight as possible and let Him do the preaching. From that day to this, preaching has been the joy of my life; I'd rather preach than eat. Sometimes when I rise to preach, before I have uttered a word, the thought of Him standing beside me, able and willing to take charge of the whole meeting and do whatever needs to be done, has so filled my heart with exultant joy that I can scarcely refrain from shouting.

Just so in your Sunday School teaching. Some of you worry about your Sunday School class for fear you will say something you ought not to say, or leave unsaid something you ought to say, and the thought of the burden and responsibility almost crushes you. Listen! Always remember this, as you sit there teaching your class: There is One right beside you Who knows just what ought to be said and just what ought to be done. Instead of carrying the responsibility of the class let Him do it, let Him do the teaching.

One Monday morning I met one of the most faithful laymen I ever knew, and a very gifted Bible teacher. This

Monday morning as I called upon him at his store he was greatly cast down over the failure in his class, or what he regarded as failure. He unburdened his heart to me, and I listened. Then when he had finished I said to him, " Mr. Dyer, did you not ask God to give you wisdom as you went before that class?" He said, " I did." Then I said, " Did you not expect Him to give it?" He replied, " I did." Then I said, " What right have you to doubt that He did?" He answered, " I never thought of that before. I will never worry about my class again."

Just so in your personal work. When I or someone else urges you at the close of the meeting to go and speak to someone else, Oh, how often you want to go, but you do not stir. You think to yourself, " I might say the wrong thing. I might do more harm than good." Well, you will say the wrong thing if you say it. Yes, if you say it you certainly will say the wrong thing, but trust the Holy Spirit to do the talking and He will say the right thing through you. Let Him have your lips to speak through. It may not appear to be the right thing at the time, but sometime you will find that it was just the right thing.

One night in Launceston, Tasmania, as Mrs. Torrey and I went away from the meeting my wife said to me, " Archie, I wasted the whole evening. I have been talking to the most frivolous girl you ever saw. I don't think she had a serious thought in her head, and I spent the whole evening with her." I replied, " Clara, how do you know that you wasted the evening? Did you not ask God to guide you?" "Yes." "Did you not expect Him to?" "Yes." "Well, leave it with Him." The very next night at the close of the meeting the same seemingly utterly frivolous young woman came up to Mrs. Torrey, leading her mother by the hand, and said, "Mrs. Torrey, won't you speak to my mother? You led me to Christ last night, now please lead my mother to Christ."

But I must close. There is another line of proof of the Personality of the Holy Spirit, but we have no time to dwell upon it.

To sum it all up: The Holy Spirit is a Person. Theoretically we probably all believed that before, but do you in your real thought of Him, in your practical attitude toward Him, treat Him as a Person? Do you really regard the Holy Spirit as just as real a person as Jesus Christ, just as loving, just as wise, just as tender, just as strong, just as faithful, just as worthy of your confidence and your love, and surrender as He? Do you think of Him as a Divine Person always at your side? The Holy Spirit was sent by the Father into this world to be to the disciples of our Lord in this present dispensation, after our Lord's departure and until His return, to be to you and me, just what Jesus Christ had been to His disciples during the days of His personal companionship with them on earth. Is He that to you? Do you know " *the communion* of the Holy Spirit?" the companionship of the Holy Spirit, the partnership of the Holy Spirit, the fellowship of the Holy Spirit, the comradeship of the Holy Spirit? To put it all into a single word, I say it reverently, the whole object of this address is to introduce you to my Friend, the Holy Spirit.

II

THE HOLY SPIRIT CONVINCING MEN OF SIN

YESTERDAY afternoon we studied together about the Holy Spirit as a Person, the Holy Spirit Himself. Today we begin a study of the work of the Holy Spirit, and we shall begin our study of His work just where He begins His work in most of us. Will you please turn in your Bibles to John, the sixteenth chapter, the seventh to the eleventh verses:

" Nevertheless I tell you the truth: It is expedient for you that I go away: for if I go not away, the Comforter will not come unto you; but if I go, I will send Him unto you. And *He, when He is come, will convict the world in respect of sin,* and *of righteousness,* and *of judgment:* of sin, *because they believe not on Me;* of righteousness, *because I go to the Father,* and ye behold Me no more; of judgment, *because the prince of this world hath been judged.*"

In these verses we are told that, *It is the work of the Holy Spirit to " Convict the world in respect of sin, and of righteousness, and of judgment."*

I. THE HOLY SPIRIT CONVICTING THE WORLD OF SIN

First of all, *It is the work of the Holy Spirit to convict men of sin.* That is to say, it is the work of the Holy Spirit to show men their error concerning sin in such a

41

way as to produce a deep sense of personal sinfulness. This is where the work of salvation begins in most men, they are brought to realize that they are sinners and that, therefore, they need a Saviour, and then they are ready without much urging to accept Jesus Christ as their Saviour, when He is presented to them as just the all-sufficient Saviour they so sorely need.

One of the great needs of the present day is conviction of sin. The average man has no realization of the awfulness of sin, nor of the fact that he himself is a great sinner before God. If men and women can be brought to a realization of what great sinners they are before God, most of their doctrinal difficulties about the Deity of Christ and about the doctrine of the atonement *through the shed blood of Jesus Christ,* will take care of themselves; for nothing but a *Divine* Saviour Who has redeemed them *by shedding His blood to pay the penalty of their sins* will satisfy the longings of their own hearts. This is one of the greatest lacks in much of our so-called " revival work " today, the lack of a deep sense of sin on the part of those who come, or profess to come, to Jesus Christ.

Now it is the work of the Holy Spirit to thus convict men of sin, to bring them to a realization of their sinfulness, and of their lost condition, and of their great guilt before God. Neither you nor I can convince any man of sin. As we shall see later, the Holy Spirit uses us to do the work, that is, He does the work through us, but we of ourselves cannot do it. He must do it. The human heart is " deceitful above all things, and desperately wicked " (Jer. 17:9), and there is nothing in which the deceitfulness of the human heart comes out more clearly than in the blindness of every one of us to our own sinfulness.

We are very sharp-sighted as regards the sins and short-comings of others, but very blind to our own. And the world is so blind to its sinfulness that no one but the Holy Spirit can ever convince the world of sin, that is, can ever bring men to see how sinful they are. No matter how great our natural powers of reasoning and persuasion may be, we cannot produce real conviction of sin by all our arguments and all our pathetic stories. We can get men to cry by telling pathetic stories (and by singing songs about "Tell Mother I'll Be There"), but *mere shedding of tears over pathetic stories and touching songs is not conviction of sin.* REAL CONVICTION OF SIN CAN ONLY BE PRODUCED BY THE HOLY SPIRIT.

Here is where many of us make our greatest mistake both in our preaching and in our personal work; we try to convince men of sin, we try to do the Holy Spirit's work, we try to do what He alone can do, and of course we fail.

I had a very striking illustration of this some years ago in our own church in Chicago. One night one of our very best workers came to me in the after-meeting and said, "I have a man over here, an engineer on the Pan-handle Railroad. I want you to talk with him. I have been talking with him for two straight hours and have made no impression upon him. Won't you come and speak with him?" I went over and she introduced me to the man, and I sat down beside him and began to use the Word of God to produce conviction of sin, but all the time looking to the Holy Spirit to carry His own Word home. I had not talked with him ten minutes when the man was under deep conviction of sin and down on his knees crying to God for mercy. While I had talked with him this lady who had been talking with him for two hours had listened. As a rule that is a very unwise thing to do, for one worker to listen while another talks with an inquirer; for men will not open their hearts, nor will they get the real help they need while a third party is listening. But this woman had a purpose in doing it, and it was all right in this instance. When the man had gone out the worker turned to me and said, " Mr. Torrey, that is very strange." I said, " What is strange?" She replied, " Do you know that you used exactly the same passages of Scripture in dealing with that man that I used, and I talked with him two hours and made no impression, and you talked with him not more than ten minutes and he was under conviction of sin and crying to God for mercy? "

Now, really, there was no mystery about it, nothing strange about it. What was the explanation? I believe it was this, that that worker for once had made a mistake that she seldom made, that of trying to do the Holy Spirit's work, trying to convince of sin the man with whom she was dealing. And when she came to me and said, " I have talked with this man two hours and made no impression upon him," the thought came to me at once, " If Miss W——, one of my best workers, has talked with this man for two hours and made no impression, what is the use of my trying to talk with him"; and in a sense of utter helplessness I had cast myself upon God, upon the Holy Spirit, to do the work, and He had done it.

Oh, let us never forget that it is impossible for us to convince any man or woman of sin, and in all our preaching and in all our personal work let us constantly look to the Holy Spirit to do the work through us; and let us also be sure that we are in such relations to God that the Holy Spirit can do His work through us.

But while we cannot convince men of sin, while it is utterly impossible for us to do it, thank God, the Holy Spirit can do it. And, if we would put ourselves at the disposal of the Holy Spirit for Him to use us as He will, and if we would look to the Holy Spirit to convince men of sin through us, and if we would be more careful to be in such relations with God that the Holy Spirit can work through us, we would see far more conviction of sin than we do.

When I was pastor of the Moody Church in Chicago, we had a committee of the church, composed of something like twenty-five members, consisting of the elders and deacons and other officers of the church, who met together for supper every Friday night, and after supper went over the roll of the church, keeping a constant watch-care of the members of the church, and discussed the various business matters of the Church. At one of these Friday night meetings, after we had been discussing various important matters, one of our elders said, " Brethren, I am not at all satisfied with the way things are going in our church. We are having many professed conversions, and we are having many accessions to the Church, but I do not see the conviction of sin that I would like to see, and I propose that, instead of discussing business matters any further tonight, we spend the time in prayer, and that we meet on other nights also, to cry to God to send His Holy Spirit among us in convicting power." The whole committee saw the wisdom of the suggestion, and it was immediately adopted ; and the remainder of that meeting was spent in prayer, and for a number of nights we met together for prayer, to pray definitely for the convicting power of the Holy Spirit in the work of the church.

Not long after that, one Sunday night, when I arose to

preach I looked around to my left and saw sitting in the front seat underneath the gallery, right beside one of my deacons, a large, well-dressed man, rather over-dressed, with a great big diamond shining from his shirt front. Something about the man's appearance led me to say to myself, " I believe that man is a sporting man." It turned out later that he was. His mother kept a sporting-house in Omaha and he himself was in Chicago at that time, gambling. I said to myself as I saw him sitting there beside the deacon, " Deacon Young has been fishing to-day."—It is a great thing to have deacons in your church who go fishing on Sunday, fishing for souls.—Every now and then as I preached I would look around at that man. His eyes were riveted upon me, he was evidently deeply interested. When I went down-stairs to the after-meeting, I noticed that Deacon Young had brought him down to the after-meeting, and when I went into an inner room for a little closer dealing with individuals, I saw that Deacon Young brought him in there. We were a long time dealing with souls that night, and about eleven o'clock I had just finished dealing with the last one I expected to speak to, when Deacon Young came over to me and said, " I've got a man over here I want you to talk with." I went over; it was this big sporting man. He was greatly agitated. " Oh," he groaned as Deacon Young introduced me to him, " I don't know what's the matter with me. I feel awful."

Then he went on to tell me this story. He said, " My mother keeps a sporting-house in Omaha, and I am here gambling in Chicago. This is the first time that I was ever in a Protestant service in my life. I started out this afternoon to go down to Cottage Grove Avenue to meet some friends down there, and to spend the afternoon gambling. But I was passing by Washington Square over yonder and some of the young men of your church were holding a meeting in the open air. Among them I saw a man named Forbes whom I had known in a life of sin, and I said to myself, 'I wonder what Forbes is doing in a meeting like this,' and I stopped to listen to what he might have to say. I was not much impressed and started down the street to go to Cottage Grove Avenue. I had gone about two blocks when some mysterious power took hold of me and brought me back to that meeting. When the meeting was over this gentleman (pointing to Deacon Young) got hold of me and took me to your Yoke Fellows' meeting for supper, and to the meeting that followed the supper, and then took me to the meeting up-stairs, and then brought me down here." And then he uttered a groan, " Oh, I don't know what's the matter with me. I never felt like this before. I feel awful," and he trembled like a leaf and groaned. I said, " I'll tell you what's the matter with you. The Holy Spirit is convicting you of sin." And that powerful man, shaking and trembling with deep emotion, that man who had never been in a Protestant service before in all his life, got down on his knees and cried to God for mercy, and went out with the joyous realization that his sins were all forgiven.

Oh, that is what we want to see in our meetings. That is what we can see if we only realize our own utter inability to convince men of sin, and believe in the power of the Holy Spirit to do it, and look to Him to do it, and depend upon Him to do it, and count upon Him to do it, and be sure that we ourselves are in such relations to God that He can do it through us.

Let me give you another illustration of the convicting,

power of the Holy Spirit. Another Sunday night, when I arose to preach in the Moody Church, as I looked up into the gallery to my left, I saw, almost directly over where the other man had sat, another very loudly-dressed man. He, too, had a great diamond shining from his shirt front, and I said to myself, " Ah, there is another sporting man." It turned out that he was a travelling man, but he was also a sporting man. As I preached, he listened with the closest attention and kept moving farther and farther to the front edge of his seat, his eyes fastened on me. In the midst of my sermon, with no intention whatever of drawing the net at that time, but merely to drive a point home, I said, " Who will take Jesus Christ right now? " The words had scarcely left my lips when he sprang to his feet and his voice rang out through the church like a pistol shot, " I will." I stopped preaching right then and there—I was not there to save sermons, but to save souls—and I gave the invitation to all who would accept Jesus Christ as their Saviour right then and there to rise to their feet, and all over the house men and women and young people sprang to their feet.

I remember one man especially, an old colonel from New York City, belonging to one of the richest families in New York City, but whose family had sent him out to Chicago to drink himself to death, and that was exactly what he was doing in one of the Chicago hotels. He was present at our service that night, a man over seventy years of age. He was one of the first men on his feet, with the tears running down his rugged cheeks, and he too accepted Christ that night.

But the Holy Spirit has power, not merely to convict of sin men and women who have wandered far from God, such as I have just described; He has power to produce the deepest conviction of sin in the hearts of people of culture and refinement, men and women living upright lives, men and women of most attractive and winsome personality.

I was sitting one day in my office in the Bible Institute in Chicago, waiting for the dinner-bell to ring, when there came a rap at my door. " Come in," I said, and there entered an old Scotch gentleman of the finest type. He was a man over eighty years of age. I showed him to a chair and almost immediately he burst into tears. Then he said to me: " You do not know me but I know you. I come constantly to hear you preach, and I have come around today to ask you if you think there is any hope for a sinner who has sinned so greatly, and continued so long in sin, as I have." Seldom have I seen a man under deeper conviction of sin than this elderly gentleman who had always lived an upright life; but who had never accepted Christ. I took my Bible and showed him, on the one hand, what the Bible had to say about him and his exceeding sinfulness, and what it had to say, on the other side, about the Lord Jesus Christ, the Son of God, Who came down into this world to save him, and upon Whom all his sins had been laid, and in Whose atoning death he might then and there find pardon, and Who had risen again and was now a living Saviour " able to save to the uttermost " anyone who came to God through Him. And this fine old Scotch gentleman knelt with me in prayer and accepted the Lord Jesus as his own Saviour and went out of my office rejoicing in the knowledge that his sins were all forgiven.

Some years ago I was attending a Bible Conference in Atlanta in the Baptist Tabernacle. At the close of one of my addresses, a prominent Baptist preacher, a scholarly man, asked for a private interview with me. This minister was a graduate of a leading Southern university. After graduating from the university he had taken a course at the Louisville Theological Seminary, and after that had gone to Chicago University for post-graduate study and had made so fine a record there that he had been sent to Germany to represent the University there. He was now pastor of a leading Baptist church in Georgia. He said to me: " I have a difficult problem on hand and I wish your advice. I am the pastor of a church in a university town. My congregation is largely made up of university professors and their families and university students. They are charming people. Some of them put me to shame by the beauty of their lives." " Now," he continued, " if I had a congregation such as they have in the Pacific Garden Mission in Chicago of down-and-outs and bums and men like that, it would be easy to convict them of sin (that is where he was mistaken), but my problem is how to convict of sin people of the beautiful character and conduct that constitute my audiences." " You cannot do it," I replied, " but the Holy Spirit can."

Oh, is not that what we need to see in our meetings here? Is that not what we need to see in our regular services in our churches? Is that not what we most need to see over all our land today in all our efforts to lead men to a better life,—deep conviction of sin wrought by the power of the Holy Ghost? Well, He can do it; He alone can do it. He can do it just as well today as He ever could; and He will if we only look to Him to do it. It was He that did it on the Day of Pentecost, when three thousand men and women were pricked in their heart and cried aloud to the apostles, " Men and brethren, what shall we do?" If Peter had preached that same sermon the day before Pentecost, the day before the Holy Spirit came, there would have been no such results; but now he and the hundred twenty "*were all filled with the Holy Spirit*" (Acts 2:4), and he preached, and the others did personal work, *in the power of the Spirit of God* and *therefore* those wonderful results followed. Oh, we to-day need to believe in the Holy Spirit and believe in His power to convict men of sin, and we need to realize our utter dependence upon Him and to cast ourselves upon Him, and look to Him to do His glorious work; and then He surely will do it.

Now will you notice just what sin it is of which the Holy Spirit convicts men. Let me read it to you again. "And He, when He is come, will convict the world in respect of sin . . . of sin, *because they believe not on me.*" The sin of which the Holy Spirit convicts men and women is the sin of unbelief in Jesus Christ: not the sin of drunkenness, not the sin of stealing, not the sin of adultery, not the sin of murder, nor of any other immorality or crime, *but just the sin of not believing on the Son of God, not believing on Jesus Christ.*

This was the sin of which the Holy Spirit convicted the three thousand on the Day of Pentecost. The Apostle Peter had just said in Acts 2:36, "Therefore let all the house of Israel know assuredly, that God hath made that same Jesus, whom ye have crucified, both Lord and Christ." Then we read in the thirty-seventh verse, "Now when they heard this (that is, had heard that the One whom they had rejected was both Lord and Christ), they were pricked in their heart, and said unto Peter and to the rest of the apostles, Men and brethren, What shall we do?" Yes, this is the sin of which the Holy Spirit convinces men and women today, the sin, the awful sin, of rejecting Him, of not believing in Him, Whom God hath made our Divine " Lord and Christ."

Now that is the very sin of which it is most difficult to convince men. The average unbeliever does not look upon his unbelief in Jesus Christ as sin at all. Oftentimes he is proud of his unbelief, instead of being ashamed of it; and he looks upon it as a mark of intellectual superiority. He struts around and says, " Oh, I am an agnostic," or, " Oh, I am a Unitarian," or, " Oh, I am a sceptic," or, " Oh, I am an infidel." Oftentimes they are all the more proud of it because it is about the only mark of intellectual superiority that they possess. If it is not quite as bad as that, and people are not proud of their unbelief, at the very worst they regard it as a mere misfortune and they will say, " Oh, I can't believe. I do wish I could believe, but I can't. Won't you please pity me because I can't believe? " But when the Spirit of God comes to a man, he does not look upon unbelief in Jesus Christ as a mark of intellectual superiority, neither does he look upon it as a mere misfortune: he sees clearly that it is the worst, the most decisive, the most daring, and the most damning of all sins, and while he may bitterly regret his dishonesty or his impurity, or whatever other sins of which he may have been guilty, he sees and feels that the most awful of his sins is the sin of rejecting the glorious Son of God. He sees that no sin he can possibly commit against a fellow man can match in enormity the sin of rejecting Him Whom God has clearly shown, by raising Him from the dead, to be His own eternal Son; and Him Who gave up heaven and all its glory to come down to earth with all its shame to bear our sins in His own body on the cross. But you and I cannot make men see that; but the Holy Ghost can, and this is the sin of which the Holy Spirit convicts men, the sin of unbelief in Jesus Christ.

II. The Holy Spirit Convicting the World of Righteousness

But the Holy Spirit not only convicts men of sin, He also " Convicts the world . . . of righteousness;" not of our righteousness, for we have none, but of Jesus Christ's righteousness, attested by His resurrection from the dead and by His ascension to the Father, and the righteousness which God has provided for us in Jesus Christ.

There are two things, and two things only, that anyone needs to see in order to be saved: First, he needs to see his own sin and consequent need; Second, he needs to see the righteousness of Jesus Christ, and the righteousness which God has provided for him in Christ; and it is the work of the Holy Spirit to show men both these things.

One of the most remarkable revivals in the history of the Church, one in which the work of the Holy Spirit was most clearly and wonderfully manifested, was the Ulster Revival in the North of Ireland in the years 1859 and 1860. Rev. William Gibson, the Moderator of the General Assembly of the Presbyterian Church of Ireland, in the year 1860, has written a very full history of that revival, and in it he relates many instances of conversion. They were all typical: men and women were brought under overwhelming conviction of sin; sometimes this conviction of sin lasted for days (that, of course, was unnecessary if Christ had been properly presented at once); then after days of deep and awful conviction the light would break in upon men and they would get a wonderful view of Jesus Christ and just believe on Him, and enter into a clear experience of forgiveness of sin.

and of wonderful joy in the Lord. It was simply the Holy Spirit convincing men of sin, and also convincing them of righteousness.

Some years ago I was at the meeting of the Men's Brotherhoods of the United Presbyterian Church of America, held at Pittsburgh. I spoke upon the subject of prayer, and in my address used as an illustration the Ulster Revival. A gentleman, a member of the church where the meetings were held, had sent his limousine to my hotel to take me to the meeting, but he had not come himself; but just sent his chauffeur. When I went out of the meeting that afternoon to hurry to another meeting, the gentleman himself was at the door and said, " I am going to ride back with you." We had scarcely gotten into the automobile when he turned to me and said, " I was converted in that Ulster Revival of which you were speaking. I was a mere lad. I was out in the field and I was ridiculing the revival, and suddenly I was struck to the ground and fairly wallowed in the furrow, overwhelmed with the sense of my sinfulness. And then, as I wallowed there in the furrow, I was given a wonderful view of Jesus Christ dying for my sins, and I believed on Him and was saved before I arose out of the furrow."

Oh, that is what we need here in these meetings, men and women brought under overwhelming conviction of sin by the Holy Spirit, then the Holy Spirit revealing Christ to them, convincing them of righteousness, the righteousness of Christ and the righteousness which God has provided for us in Jesus Christ.

The story is told of a faithful Scotch minister who was travelling through Scotland and stopped one night at an inn. The innkeeper came to him and asked him if he would conduct family worship. He replied that he would if the innkeeper on his part would bring to the worship all the guests in the house, and all the servants.   This the innkeeper agreed to do.   When they were gathered in the big room for the service the minister turned to the innkeeper and said, " Are all the servants here ? "   " Yes," replied the innkeeper.   " All ? " persisted the minister. " Well, not all.   All but one.   There is one girl who works down in the kitchen washing the pots and kettles, who is so dirty that she is not fit to come to the meeting." The minister replied, " We will not go on with the service until she comes," and he insisted and the innkeeper went for this servant and brought her in.   This faithful man of God became greatly interested in this poor, neglected creature ; and when the others were passing out of the room he asked her if she would not stay for a few minutes.   And when everyone had gone he said to her, " I want to teach you a prayer for you to offer : ' Lord, show me myself.'   Will you offer it every day ? "   She replied that she would.   The next day the minister left, but a short time afterward came back again and asked the innkeeper about this girl.   The innkeeper replied, " She is spoiled, she is no good at all.   She is weeping all the time, weeping day and night, and can hardly attend to her work."   The minister asked to see her again, and when she came in the minister said, " Now I want to teach you another prayer.   ' Lord, show me thyself.'   Now pray that prayer every day."

The minister left and a few years afterward was preaching one Lord's Day morning in a church in Glasgow.   At the close of the service a neat, trim looking young woman came up to him and said, " Do you recognize me ? "   He replied, " No, I do not."   She said, " Do you recall holding a service in an inn and speaking to one of the servants afterward, and teaching her to pray the prayer, 'Lord, show me myself,' and afterward teaching her the other prayer, 'Lord, show me Thyself'?" "Oh, yes," he said, "I remember that." "Well," she said, "I am that girl. And when you taught me that first prayer and went away, and I asked God to show me myself, He gave me such a view of my vileness and my sin that I was overwhelmed with grief and could scarcely sleep at night or work by day for thinking of my sins. Then," she said, "when you came back and taught me the second prayer, 'Lord, show me Thyself,' God gave me such a view of Himself, of His love and of Jesus Christ dying on the cross for me, that all the burden of my sin rolled away and I became a happy Christian." Yes, those are the two things that each one of us needs to see—our own sin, and it is the work of the Holy Spirit to show us that, and the righteousness of Christ and the righteousness that God has provided for you and me in Jesus Christ, and it is the work of the Holy Spirit to show us that also.

III. The Holy Spirit Convincing the World of Judgment

But *there is still a third thing of which the Holy Spirit convicts men, and that is of judgment,* attested by the judgment of the prince of this world, the Devil. There has perhaps never been a day in the whole history of the Church of Jesus Christ on earth when the world needed more to be convinced of " judgment," than today. The average man has but little faith that there is to be a future judgment. Indeed, a large number of our church members, and even of our preachers, have lost all realization of future judgment and of a future awful hell. A great many of our churches, and not a few of our superficially orthodox preachers, have really given up all belief in such a hell as Jesus Christ and the Bible taught, and even those preachers who do still believe in it theoretically seldom, if ever, preach it.

When the question was being discussed of inviting me to the city of D——, the Y. M. C. A. Secretary of that city said, " We do not want Dr. Torrey to hold evangelistic services in D——, for he will preach hell, and we do not wish to have hell preached here in D——." Now he had sized me up exactly right. I certainly would preach hell, for Jesus Christ preached it, and God, in our day as well as in all other days, greatly blesses the preaching of His truth. It is only fair to say that when I actually did go to that city, that same secretary was about the most faithful supporter that I had in the city. But his remark at that time shows the attitude that many take today on this subject. Many think that while the doctrine of eternal punishment is true, that it ought not to be taught because it is not what men like to hear today; just as though what men liked to hear is what they ought to hear. Very frequently the truth that men least like to hear is the truth that they most need to hear.

When I was holding meetings in the city of Philadelphia, in the North Armory, I preached two sermons on hell. A few nights afterward, as I was going out of the armory to get into the carriage to take me to my home about three miles away, I saw a Presbyterian minister who had a church near my home going out of the armory, and I invited him to get into the carriage with my daughter and myself and we would take him home. After we had ridden some distance, this minister turned to me and said, " Dr. Torrey, one of my elders asked me a question the other day. He asked me if I believed in hell the way you preached it. I replied, 'Have you any reason for suspecting that I don't?' 'No,' he said, 'I have no reason for suspecting that you don't, but do you?' Then I replied, 'Yes, I do. I believe every word that Dr. Torrey preached on the subject.' Then my elder said, 'Then why don't you preach it?'" Yes, why don't we preach it? We certainly need to preach it. The world needs to hear it, and God blesses the preaching of it.

Now when the Spirit of God comes to men they believe in " judgment." I doubt if any minister ever had more difficulties with the doctrine of future punishment as taught in the Bible than I did. I would come up to this doctrine time and time again, and would back off every time I came up to it. In my early ministry I succeeded in convincing myself that the Bible did not teach everlasting punishment, that while it taught that there would be a hell, and an awful hell, and a hell that might last through centuries or even thousands of years, that at last " somehow, somewhere, somewhen," all men, and even the Devil himself, would be brought to repentance and hell would therefore cease to be. So I believed and so I taught. But the time came when I could no longer reconcile the teachings of the Bible with this position, and so I gave it up, and theoretically I believed in an everlasting hell; but even after that, every time I came up to the doctrine, as I say, I would back off, it seemed as if I could not possibly have it that way. But one night, after I had gone to Chicago I was waiting upon God that I might know the Holy Spirit in a fuller way than I had ever known Him before, that I might be " baptized with the Holy Spirit " in a more thorough-going way than I ever had been before. And that night God heard my prayer, and such a filling with the Holy Spirit, such a being taken possession of by the Holy Spirit, as I had never known before, came to me, and with that new infilling of the Holy Spirit there came such a revelation of the infinite majesty and glory of Jesus Christ, the wondrous Son of God, and such a revelation of the awfulness of the sin of rejecting such a glorious Saviour as that, that I saw at once that if men would not accept this glorious Saviour, then all the most terrible statements to be found in the Word of God as to the future eternal destiny of those who would not accept Jesus Christ, were demanded by the very necessities of the case, and from that day to this I have never had the slightest difficulty with the doctrine of future punishment taught in the Bible. The Holy Spirit Himself had convinced me of judgment. God grant that He may you also.

IV. The Holy Spirit Convinces the World Only Through Believers in Jesus Christ

To sum it all up then; it is the work of the Holy Spirit to convict men of sin, and of righteousness, and of judgment. It is not our work, but His. But please notice very carefully that, WHILE IT IS THE HOLY SPIRIT WHO CONVICTS MEN OF SIN, AND OF RIGHTEOUSNESS, AND OF JUDGMENT, HE DOES IT THROUGH US, *i. e.*, THROUGH THOSE WHO ALREADY BELIEVE ON JESUS CHRIST. This thought comes out in the seventh and eighth verses: "Nevertheless I tell you the truth: It is expedient for you that I go away; for if I go not away, the Comforter will not come *unto you;* but if I go, I will send Him *unto you* (that is, to believers). And He, when He is come (that is, come unto you, come unto believers), will *convict the world* in respect of sin, and of righteousness, and of judgment," that is to say, the Holy Spirit comes to the believer, and through the believer to whom He comes convinces the unsaved. *As far as we are told in the Bible, the Holy Spirit has no way of getting at the unsaved except through the channel of those who are already saved;* He comes to the believer and through the believer convinces the unsaved of sin. What a solemn thought that is. If we realized that the Holy Spirit could only reach the unbeliever through us, us who are already saved, would we not be more careful to present to the Holy Spirit an unchoked channel for the Holy Spirit to work through?

Every conversion recorded in the Acts of the Apostles was through human instrumentality, not one single conversion is recorded there that was not by human instrumentality. Take, for example, the conversion of Cornelius. If there was ever a miraculous conversion it was that! Why, we are told in the tenth chapter of the Acts of the Apostles that an angel appeared to Cornelius and spoke to him, but the angel did not tell Cornelius what to do to be saved. On the contrary, the angel said to him, " Send men to Joppa, and call for one Simon, whose surname is Peter; who shall tell thee words whereby thou and all thy house shall be saved " (Acts 11:13, 14). In other words, not even an angel could show him the way of life, it must be a saved fellow-man, and a Spirit-filled fellow-man, who did it.

Take the conversion of Saul of Tarsus. If ever there was a miraculous conversion it was certainly that, when the risen and ascended Lord Jesus Himself appeared to him, he actually saw Jesus in the glory, but the Lord Jesus did not tell him what to do to be saved. Paul cried, " What shall I do, Lord? " (Acts 22:10). And the Lord said unto him, " Arise and go into Damascus, and *there it shall be told thee* of all things which are appointed for thee to do." The Lord did not tell him what to do to be saved, "a certain" man "named Ananias" had to be brought upon the scene, and Ananias told him what to do, saying, "Arise, and be baptized, and wash away thy sins, calling on the name of the Lord" (Acts 9:10; 22:16).

As far as God tells us in His Word, THE HOLY GHOST HAS NO WAY OF GETTING AT THE UNSAVED WORLD EXCEPT THROUGH US WHO ARE ALREADY SAVED. This is exceedingly solemn. Oh, if we only realized it, would we not be more careful to present to the Holy Spirit an unobstructed channel for Him to work through! Do you take that in? Does it mean you?

You wives who have unconverted husbands. You are praying for their conversion, you are praying that God will send His Holy Spirit to convict them of sin and show them their need of Christ; but the Holy Spirit can get at them only through some saved person, and most likely only through you, for you are the nearest to them. And many and many a man is lost because his wife is such an obstructed channel that the Holy Spirit cannot work through her, and so her husband is lost forever.

One time when Mr. Moody was holding meetings in Philadelphia a lady came to him and asked him to pray for her husband. He replied, "No, I'll not pray for your husband." "What!" she exclaimed, "not pray for my husband? Do you not pray for the unsaved?" "Yes, I do, but I will not pray for *your* husband." "Why not?" she asked. "Because," Mr. Moody replied, "I believe you yourself are the greatest obstacle there is in the way of the conversion of your husband." The woman was greatly provoked and went to her husband after she

got home and said, " Mr. Moody insulted me this afternoon." " What," replied her husband, " Mr. Moody insulted you? I thought Mr. Moody was a gentleman, I
did not suppose he would insult any lady." " Yes,"
she replied, " Mr. Moody insulted me this afternoon."
" What did Mr. Moody say to you? " her husband asked.
" He said I was the greatest obstacle there was in the
way of your conversion." " Well, ain't you? " said her
husband. And some of you wives here today who are
trying to get people to pray for the conversion of your
husband, you who are deeply concerned for the conversion of your husband, you yourself are the greatest obstacle there is in the way of the conversion of your husband. The Holy Spirit has no way of getting at your
husband except through you, and unless you get thoroughly right with God yourself and become an unobstructed channel through which the Holy Spirit can work,
your husband will be lost forever.

When I was holding meetings in Omaha, the pastor of
the leading Methodist Church in the city became deeply
concerned about the salvation of one of the most prominent members of his congregation, a leading business
man, and he called upon him at his store. The gentleman
invited Dr. S—— up to his private office, and Dr. S——
commenced to talk to him about his soul. The man
listened and then said, " Dr. S——, what do you want
me to be like? Do you want me to be like my wife, she
is a member of your church? Do you want me to be like
her? I have seen her greatly excited over a whist drive.
I have never seen her nearly so excited over a prayer-
meeting in all her life as I have seen her over a whist
drive. Do you want me to be like her? "

But then again there are many of us who will not even

offer ourselves at all to the Holy Spirit as an instrument for Him to work through.   Oh, how many there are here in this audience today whose lips the Holy Spirit is trying to get the use of, but you will not give Him the use of your lips.   He is trying to reach someone through you, but you will not allow Him to.

I once read of a young lady who died in New York City. A Presbyterian minister was invited to conduct the funeral services; he was not her own pastor; I do not know why her own pastor was not invited. This minister who was to conduct the services went first to her own pastor and asked him, "Was Mary a Christian?" Her pastor replied, "I do not know. Three weeks ago I had a very solemn impression that I ought to speak to Mary about her soul, but I put it off. I said, 'Mary is in my congregation every Sunday and I can speak to her when I will,' and I put it off and now Mary is dead and I do not know whether Mary was a Christian or not." He next went to her Sunday School teacher and asked her Sunday School teacher, "Was Mary a Christian?" The Sunday School teacher replied, "I do not know. Two weeks ago I had a profound impression that I ought to speak to Mary about her soul, but I put it off. I said, 'Mary is in my class every Sunday and I can speak to her when I will,' and I put it off. And now Mary is dead and I don't know whether Mary was a Christian or not." He next went to her own mother and said to her, "Was Mary a Christian?" "I do not know. A week ago I had a deep impression that I ought to speak to Mary about her soul, but I put it off. I said, 'Here is Mary in the house with me all the time. I meet her three times a day at the table. I can speak to her when I will,' and I put it off, and now Mary is dead and I do not know

whether Mary was a Christian or not." Three pairs of
lips that the Holy Spirit was trying to get the use of, the
three pairs of lips that one would naturally think would
be most easily at His disposal, her minister's, her Sunday
School teacher's and her mother's, and not one of the
three would let the Holy Spirit have the use of their lips,
and so Mary died unsaved. When I got back from going
around the world and spent a month with my church in
Chicago, I related this incident one Sunday morning.
There was in my audience a young woman who had a
class of girls from about fourteen years of age up. What
I said made a deep impression upon her, and when she
went before her class that Sunday afternoon she spoke
to every member of her class about accepting Christ.
Among those who did accept Christ was a girl fourteen
years of age, if I remember correctly, apparently perfectly well and strong. Before the next Sunday came
round that girl's body was lying out in the cemetery.
Oh, how fortunate that that young woman that morning
gave her lips to Jesus Christ to use. Have you given
yours? And are you listening for the Holy Spirit to
show you to whom to go? And are you depending upon
the Holy Spirit to work through you? And are you an
unobstructed channel?

Let me beseech you, every one of you that professes
to be a Christian, to put your lips today at the Holy
Spirit's disposal for Him through you to convict whom-
soever He will of sin, and of righteousness, and of
judgment. And be sure that you are fully surrendered
to God and that you have thoroughly put out of your
life everything that would hinder the Holy Spirit work-
ing through you, and that you are an unobstructed
channel for the Holy Spirit to work through; and be

listening, listening sharply, for the Holy Spirit's directions as to whom to speak.

When Mr. Alexander and I were holding meetings in Brighton, England, in the great Dome, one afternoon one of our workers went away from the afternoon meeting and went into a restaurant for tea before coming back to the night meeting. While he was sitting at the table he had a deep impression that he ought to speak to the waiter about his soul, but he put it off. It seemed to him as if it would be a strange thing to speak to a man who was waiting upon him about accepting Christ. He finished his meal and went outside, but his impression that he should have spoken to that waiter was so deep that he waited outside for the waiter to come out, intending to talk to him then. When he had waited there for some time, the proprietor of the restaurant came out and began to put up the shutters, and asked him what he was waiting for. He replied, " I am waiting to speak to that man that waited upon me at the table." The proprietor said, " You will never speak to that man again. Immediately after serving you he went up to his room and blew his brains out." Oh, men and women, we live in a solemn world, and we need to be very careful how we walk. We need to be ready for God to use us any moment, and to respond to His call. THE HOLY SPIRIT ALONE CONVINCES MEN OF SIN, AND OF RIGHTEOUSNESS, AND OF JUDGMENT; BUT HE DOES IT THROUGH US—never forget that.

III

THE REGENERATING WORK OF THE HOLY SPIRIT

YESTERDAY we were studying the work of the Holy Spirit in convicting men of sin. We saw that it was the work of the Holy Spirit to convict men of sin and of righteousness and of judgment. Today we shall study further the work of the Holy Spirit.

I. THE HOLY SPIRIT BEARING WITNESS TO THE TRUTH REGARDING JESUS CHRIST

Turn first of all to Jno. 15:26, 27: "But when the Comforter is come, whom I will send unto you from the Father, even the Spirit of truth, which proceedeth from the Father, He *shall bear witness of Me:* and ye also bear witness because ye have been with Me from the beginning." Here we see that *it is the work of the Holy Spirit to bear witness concerning Jesus Christ.* All the work of the Holy Spirit centres in Jesus Christ. It is His work to magnify Christ to us, *to glorify Christ* by taking of the things of Christ and declaring them unto us (cf. ch. 16:14).

It is only through the direct testimony of the Holy Spirit in the individual heart that any man ever comes to a true and living and saving knowledge of Jesus Christ (cf. 1 Cor. 12:3). No amount of listening to the testimony of men regarding Jesus Christ, and no amount even of studying what the Scriptures have to say about Christ Jesus, will ever lead anyone to a true and living and saving knowledge of Jesus Christ unless the Holy Spirit, the living Spirit of God, takes the testimony of men, or takes the testimony of the written Word, and interprets it directly to our hearts.

It is true that the Holy Spirit's testimony regarding Jesus Christ is found in the Bible. In fact, that is exactly what the whole Bible is, the Holy Spirit's testimony to Jesus Christ. The whole testimony of the Book centres in Jesus Christ. As we read in Rev. 19: 10, " *The testimony of Jesus* is the spirit of prophecy." But while that is true, unless the living Spirit, Who lives and works today, takes His Own testimony as it is found in the written Word, the Bible, and interprets it directly to the heart of the individual and makes it a living thing in the heart of the individual, he will not come to a real, living, saving knowledge of Jesus Christ.

If, therefore, you wish men to get a true view of Jesus Christ, such a view of Him that they will believe on Him and be saved, you must seek for them the testimony of the Holy Spirit, and you must put yourself in such relations to God that the Holy Spirit can bear His testimony through you. No amount of mere argument and persuasion on your part will ever bring anyone to a living knowledge of Jesus Christ.

And if you wish to have a true knowledge of Jesus Christ yourself, it is not enough that you study the Word and what the Spirit of God has said about Jesus Christ in the Word: you must seek for yourself the testimony of the Spirit of God directly to your own heart through His Word, and put yourself in such relations to God that the Holy Spirit can bear His testimony directly to your heart

The attitude that you must take toward God in order that the Holy Spirit may bear His testimony to Jesus Christ directly to your heart is the attitude of absolute surrender to the will of God; for Peter is recorded as saying in Acts 5:32, "We are witnesses of these things; and so is the Holy Spirit, *whom God hath given to them that obey Him.*" And we read these words of our Lord Jesus Himself in Jno. 7:17, "If any man *willeth to do His will,* he shall know of the teaching, whether it is of God, or whether I speak from Myself."

This explains why it is that one may read the Gospel of John time and time again and not come to a saving knowledge of Jesus Christ, even though that Gospel was written for the specific purpose of bringing men to a saving knowledge of Jesus Christ. The writer himself tells us in the twentieth chapter and the thirty-first verse, "These are written that ye may believe that Jesus is the Christ, the Son of God; and that believing ye may have life in His name." But if the same man will surrender his will to God before beginning to read the Gospel, and will ask God each time he reads to send His Holy Spirit to interpret to his heart the things that he reads, he cannot read the Gospel through even once, without coming to believe that Jesus is the Christ, the Son of God, and through believing "have life in His Name."

I have seen this illustrated many a time. One Sunday night as I was going out of the inquiry meeting in the Moody Church a young man was waiting for me in the vestibule. I think he had already been a Church member. He said to me, "Mr. Torrey, I don't believe anything. Can you tell me how to believe?" "Don't you believe anything at all? Don't you believe there is a God?" "Yes," he said, "I believe there is a God, but I am in doubt about everything else." "All right," I said, "if you believe there is a God you ought to surrender your will to God, then begin at the first chapter of John, first verse, read a few verses at a time, not too many, and pay close attention to what you read and each time before you read pray this prayer, 'Oh God, show me what of truth there is in these verses I am about to read, and what Thou showest me to be true I promise to take my stand upon.' And read on, day after day consecutively until you get through the Gospel. Will you do it?" "Yes," he replied, "I will." "One thing more, when you get through the Gospel, come and report to me." About two weeks after when I went out of prayer-meeting one night I met him in the vestibule again. He said, "I have come to report." I said, "What is your report?" He said, "Don't you know?" "Yes," I replied, "I think I do." "Well," he said, "my doubts are all gone. I do believe that Jesus is the Christ, the Son of God, and I do believe in the Bible as the Word of God." Why did he now believe when he did not believe before, although he had read the same book through time and time again? He believed now because he had put himself in such a relation to God that the Holy Spirit could bear His testimony through His Own written Word.

This also explains why it is that one who has been long in the darkness concerning Jesus Christ so quickly comes to see the truth, when he surrenders his will to God. It explains an experience that pretty much every thoughtful worker has had: You sit down beside an inquirer who really desires to know the truth and be saved, and you take your Bible and show him from some of the plainest statements of the Word just what one must do to be saved, namely, to believe on Jesus Christ; and you take the truth about Jesus Christ's atoning death and about His resurrection, and about His being a Deliverer from the power of sin today, and you show it to him from some of the plainest statements of the Bible along those lines; and you make the way of life as plain as day and you go over it, and over it, and over it; but still the inquirer does not see it at all but sits there dumb, puzzled, perplexed, bewildered, and he very likely tells you, " I cannot see it." Yet you have made it as plain as day. That is, to you it is as plain as day. But it is not plain to him and sometimes you are tempted to think that the inquirer is intellectually stupid. Not at all. He is perfectly clear about other things. And then you go on and on, and you go over it again and again, and suddenly a new light comes into the inquirer's face and he exclaims, " I see it—I see it," and he believes on Jesus Christ and is saved right then and there. Now what has happened? Simply this, that the Holy Spirit has borne *His* testimony directly to that inquirer's heart.

So in all our dealing with inquirers we must not only make sure that we give them the right Scripture to show them their need of a Saviour and that Jesus Christ is just the Saviour they need, *we must see to it also that we are looking to the Spirit of God to bear His witness to Jesus Christ* through us and that we are in such a relation to God that the Holy Spirit can bear His witness to Jesus Christ through us.

Take what occurred on the day of Pentecost. The Apostle Peter bore his testimony to Jesus Christ, and gave the testimony of the Old Testament Scriptures, and the Holy Spirit, through Peter's testimony and that of the Old Testament Scriptures, bore His testimony to Jesus Christ, and so men saw and believed, and in that day "there were added unto them about three thousand souls." Now, if the Apostle Peter had given just the same testimony the day before and had given just the same Scriptures the day before (that is, the day before Pentecost, the day on which the Holy Spirit was given), there would have been no such results; but the time had come for the Holy Spirit to do His work and Peter had been "filled with the Holy Spirit," "when Pentecost was fully come," and now not only did Peter give his testimony, but *the living Spirit of God,* Who had taken possession of Peter, *gave His testimony,* and men saw and believed.

Mr. Moody used to put it in this graphic way. He said: "Peter said, 'Therefore let all the house of Israel know assuredly, that God hath made that same Jesus, whom ye have crucified, both Lord and Christ' (Acts 2: 36), and the Holy Spirit said, 'Amen,' and men saw and believed."

At one time when I was superintendent of the Bible Institute in Chicago I lived in the Bible Institute, and every night I would try to get home from my own meetings before the students got home from the various places they had gone to help in the work, and I would meet them on the stairway and we would talk over the experiences of the night together. One night a large company of them came back from the Pacific Garden Mission full of enthusiasm and joy. "Oh," they said, " Mr. Torrey, we had a wonderful time at the Pacific Garden Mission tonight. Crowds of men came to the altar, all kinds of drunkards and outcasts, and were saved." The next day I met Harry Monroe, who was at that time in charge of the Pacific Garden Mission. I said, "Harry, the boys tell me you had a wonderful time at the Pacific Garden

Mission last night." He replied, " Mr. Torrey, do you want to know the secret of it? I just held up Jesus Christ and it pleased the Holy Spirit to illumine the face of Jesus as I held Him up and men saw and believed." I thought that was a beautiful way of putting it.

And so when you and I preach, or when we do personal work or teach, we should hold up Jesus Christ as He is presented in the Scriptures and then look to the Holy Spirit to illumine His face, and to be very sure we are in such a relation to God and to the Holy Spirit, and so dependent upon the Holy Spirit, and so counting upon the Holy Spirit to do His work, that He can do it, and then men will see and believe.

Let me repeat it in order that we may be sure that you get it, if you wish men to see the truth about Jesus Christ do not depend upon your own powers of expression or persuasion, or upon your own knowledge of Scripture and just how to use it, but cast yourself upon the Holy Spirit in a realization of your utter helplessness, and look to Him to bear His testimony to Jesus Christ, and see to it also that those you are dealing with put themselves in such an attitude toward God that the Holy Spirit can testify to them, and see to it also that you are in such a relation to God, so fully surrendered to Him, so separated from all that hinders His work, that He can bear His testimony through you. In the Holy Spirit's testimony to Jesus Christ lies the cure for all ignorance concerning Christ, and all scepticism concerning Christ.

II. The Holy Spirit Regenerating Men

Now let me call your attention to another wonderful, gracious and glorious work of the Holy Spirit. Turn in your Bibles to Jno. 3:3-5: " Jesus answered and said unto him (that is, unto Nicodemus), Verily, verily, I say unto thee, Except one be born again (or, "anew," or, "from above"), he cannot see the kingdom of God. Nicodemus saith unto Him, How can a man be born when he is old? can he enter a second time into his mother's womb and be born? Jesus answered, Verily, verily, I say unto thee, Except one be *born of* water and *the Spirit,* he cannot enter into the kingdom of God." Here we are told that men are born *of the Spirit, or born anew through the Holy Spirit's power.*

Exactly the same truth is set forth in a way that may enable some of you to grasp it more readily, in Titus 3:5: "Not by works done in righteousness, which we did ourselves, but according to His mercy He saved us, through the washing of regeneration and *renewing of the Holy Spirit.*" Here we are taught that *it is the work of the Holy Spirit to renew men, or to make men anew, or* (to use the common theological expression) *to regenerate men.*

WHAT IS REGENERATION? We have two definitions of "Regeneration," or "the New Birth," in the Bible. You will find the first of these definitions in Eph. 2:1: "And you did He *make alive,* when ye were dead through your trespasses and sins." *Regeneration is, then, the impartation of life to men who are morally and spiritually dead because of their trespasses and sins.* Every man and woman and child of us, no matter how excellent in character or how religious our parents may have been, was born into this world spiritually dead. We are by nature moral and spiritual corpses. In regeneration we are made alive; God imparts to us His Own life. Now it is the Holy Spirit by Whom God imparts to us this life. Regeneration is His work.

Of course the Word of God is the instrument that the

Holy Spirit uses in imparting life. That we are taught in 1 Pet. 1:23: "Having been begotten again, not of corruptible seed, but of incorruptible, through the word of God, which liveth and abideth." And we are told the same thing in Jas. 1:18: "Of His own will begat He us with the word of truth, that we should be a kind of first-fruits of His creatures." We see plainly in both of these passages that the Word of truth, the Word of God, the Word contained in the Bible, is the instrument which the Holy Spirit uses in regeneration, BUT IT IS ONLY AS THE HOLY SPIRIT USES THE WORD THAT REGENERATION RESULTS. The mere written Word will not produce the New Birth, no matter how faithfully preached or faithfully given in personal work, unless the living Spirit of God makes it a living thing in the hearts of those to whom we preach or with whom we are dealing. This comes out very plainly in another statement of the Apostle Paul's found in 2 Cor. 3:6: "The letter killeth, but the *Spirit giveth life.*" What does this mean? It is often taken in these days of superficial and careless thinking, and careless Bible study, to mean that the literal interpretation of Scripture (which these men call "the letter"), that is, taking the Scripture to mean just what it says by applying the usual laws of grammar and diction, kills, but that some spiritualizing interpretation, some interpretation that makes the Word mean something it evidently was not intended to say, that gives life. This is one of the favourite tricks in misinterpreting the Scriptures employed by those who are determined not to take the Bible as meaning what it says; and they call all those of us who insist on interpreting the Bible to mean what it says, "deadly literalists." There never was a more unwarranted misconstruction of Paul's words, or the words of anyone else, than that. Paul did not have the remotest thought of teaching anything of that kind. If there ever was a " deadly literalist " (if literalism is really deadly), it was the very man who wrote these words. Paul was always insisting upon the exact force of every word used. Paul would build a whole argument on a word, or on a part of a word, on the number of a noun, or on the case of a noun, or on the tense of a verb. No, Paul did not mean anything of that kind.

What did he mean? Well, the way to discover what any man really means by what he says or writes is to *read what he says or writes in the connection in which it is said*. In this case the connection shows beyond the possibility of honest doubt exactly what Paul meant. In the third verse of this same chapter Paul draws a contrast between the Word of God written on parchment or on paper with pen and ink, or graven on tables of stone as in the case of the Ten Commandments, and *the Word of God written* as he puts it *by " the Spirit of the living God;* not in tables of stone, but *in tables that are hearts of flesh,"* and what Paul therefore says is, that the mere " letter " of the Word, the Word written or printed in a book, kills, *i. e.,* brings condemnation and death; but that the Word of God *written by the Spirit of the living God in our hearts* (" on tables that are hearts of flesh "), that brings life. This, of course, is only to say in other words what we have already said above, that *it is only as the living Holy Spirit takes today to the heart of the individual the Word of God and writes it on the heart,* are men made alive, or born again. No amount of giving the Bible, the written Word, in sermon, or personal work, or teaching, will ever lead to a man being born again. If we wish to see men born again through our preaching, or through our personal work, or through our teaching, we must realize our dependence upon the Holy Spirit and look to Him, and count upon Him, to carry the truth that we preach or give out in personal work or in teaching, home to the heart, and see to it that we ourselves are in such a relation to God that the Holy Spirit can do His regenerating work through us.

We have a second God-given definition of Regeneration in 2 Pet. 1: 3, 4: " Seeing that His divine power hath granted unto us all things that pertain unto life and godliness, through the knowledge of Him that called us by His Own glory and virtue; whereby He hath granted unto us His precious and exceeding great promises; that through these ye *may become partakers of the divine nature,* having escaped from the corruption that is in the world by lust." *God's definition of Regeneration here is, the impartation of a new nature, " the divine nature," God's Own nature, to us.*

We are all born into this world with a corrupt nature, corrupt in its thoughts, corrupt in its affections, corrupt in its will.

1. First of all, Every one of us, no matter how fine our ancestry, or how pious our parents, are born into this world with a mind that is blind to the truth of God. As Paul puts it in 1 Cor. 2: 14, " The *natural man* receiveth not the things of the Spirit of God: for *they are foolishness unto him: neither can he know them,* because they are *spiritually discerned."*

2. In the second place, We are all of us born into this world with affections that are corrupt, that is, with affections set upon things that displease God. We love the things we ought to hate, and we hate the things we ought to love.

3. And, in the third place, We are all of us born into this world with a will that is perverse. As Paul puts it in Rom. 8:7, " *The mind of the flesh* (that is, " the mind of " the natural and unregenerate man) *is enmity against God;* for it is not subject to the law of God, neither indeed can it be." We are all of us born into this world with a will that is perverse, a will that is set upon pleasing self, and not set upon pleasing God. Now, what pleases self may not be something corrupt or criminal or vile or immoral. What pleases us may be something refined, something of a high character; it may not be getting drunk or stealing or lying or committing adultery or doing any evil or vile or base thing; it may be culture or music or art or some other high and refined thing; but *pleasing self is the very essence of sin,* whether the thing that pleases self is something very high or something very low. And any will that is set upon pleasing self is a will in rebellion against God: it is " enmity against God." There is only one right attitude for the human will, and that is an attitude of absolute surrender to God, and the whole aim of life should not be to please self at all, but to please God in all things.

So then we are all born into the world with this nature that is intellectually, affectionally and volitionally corrupt. What occurs in the New Birth? We are given a New Nature.

1. *We are given a new intellectual nature, a new mind,* a mind which instead of being blind to the truth of God is open-eyed to the truth of God. How often I have seen that. I have seen a man come into a meeting like this, an utter infidel. I have a man in mind at this moment, a man who had not been inside a church for fourteen years, and who was a rank and very bitter infidel. But this

man was induced to come and hear me preach. The Spirit of God wrought through me that night and through a personal worker who dealt with him in the after-meeting, and that man was born again then and there, and that thoroughly darkened mind became illuminated at once, and, instead of the things " of the Spirit of God " being any longer " foolishness unto him " they became as clear as day, and within a week he was bringing others into a knowledge of the truth. He brought his own wife to meeting the following Sunday night and led her into the light; and within a year he was preaching the Gospel.

2. But we are not only given a new intellectual nature, *we are also given a new affectional nature.* We get new tastes instead of the old tastes, new loves instead of the old loves. Instead of loving any longer the things that displease God we now love the things that please God. The things we once hated we now love, and the things we once loved we now hate. How clearly that was illustrated in my own experience. As I look back upon my life before I was born again I can hardly believe what I know to be true about my own affections and about my likes and my dislikes, before I was born again. In those days I hated the Bible. I read it every day, but it was to me about the most stupid Book I read, I would rather have read last year's almanac any day than to have read the Bible. But when I was born again my heart was filled with love for the Bible and today I would rather read the Bible than any other book or all books put together. I so love it that sometimes I think I will not read any other book but the Bible. In those former days, before I was born again, I loved the card-table, the theatre, the dance, the horse-race, the champagne supper, and I hated the prayer-meeting and the Sunday services.

Today I hate the dance and the card-table and the theatre and the horse-race, and I love the gathering together of God's people and the services of God's house on the Lord's Day. It is just as Paul puts it in 2 Cor. 5: 17, " If any man be in Christ, he is a new creation: the old things are passed away; behold, they are become new."

3. But *in the New Birth* we are not only given a new intellectual nature and a new affectional nature, *we are given a new volitional nature, that is, we are given a new will.* When one is born again his will is no longer set upon pleasing self: his will is set upon pleasing God. There is nothing else in which he so delights as he delights in the will of God. What he himself desires is nothing to him: what pleases God is everything to him.

We see, then, that the New Birth is the impartation of a new nature, God's Own nature, to men who are dead in trespasses and sins. *It is the Holy Spirit Who imparts this nature.* As we have already said, the Word of God is the instrument the Holy Spirit uses in imparting this new nature. This comes out in the very verse we have already quoted as containing God's definition of the New Birth, 2 Pet. 1: 4, " Whereby He hath granted unto us *His precious and exceeding great promises; that through these* (that is, through *His precious and exceeding great promises,* that is, through the written Word) ye may become partakers of the divine nature." Yes, always the written Word is the instrument through which the new nature is imparted to men, BUT IT IS ONLY AS THE HOLY SPIRIT USES THE INSTRUMENT, THE WRITTEN WORD, THAT THE NEW BIRTH, THE IMPARTATION OF GOD'S OWN NATURE TO US, RESULTS.

So we see again that if we wish to be born again ourselves, it is not enough to read the Bible, though that is the instrument the Holy Spirit uses in regeneration, we must put ourselves in such an attitude toward God, by the surrender of our will to God, that the Holy Spirit may use the written Word and make it a living thing in our hearts and thus impart God's nature to us, and thus we be born again. We see also that if we wish others to be born again through our preaching or personal work or teaching, or whatever it may be, we must see to it we not only give them the written word and give them the right passages from the Word, but that we are in such a right relation toward God, and that we so realize our dependence upon the Holy Spirit for Him to do the work, and that we so count upon Him to do the work, that He can do His regenerating work through us.

The mere letter of the Gospel will merely bring condemnation and kill, unless accompanied by the Holy Spirit's power. The ministry of many a perfectly orthodox preacher or teacher is a ministry of death; indeed one of the deadest things on earth is dead orthodoxy. His ministry is a ministry of death because while he gives the Word, he gives it "with enticing words of man's wisdom and not in demonstration of the Spirit and of power" (1 Cor. 2:4). No amount of preaching, no matter how orthodox it may be, no amount of mere study of the Word, will regenerate unless the Holy Spirit works. It is He, and He alone that makes a man a new creature. But thank God He is ever ready to do this, when the conditions are supplied which are necessary if He is to do His work. We are all dependent upon Him, if there are to be real results, real regeneration.

Just as we are utterly dependent upon the work of Christ *for* us in justification so *we are utterly dependent*

upon the work of the Holy Spirit in us for regeneration.
The whole work of regeneration can be described in this
way: the human heart is the soil, the Word of God is the
seed, we preachers and teachers and personal workers are
the sowers. We go to the granary of the Bible and take
from it that portion of seed we wish to sow; we preach
it or teach it or use it in personal work; but if it all
stopped there there would be no real result, there would
be no New Birth. But, if as we preach or teach or do
personal work, we look to the Holy Spirit to do His
work, He will quicken the seed as we sow it, and it will
take root in the hearts of those to whom we speak, and
the human heart will close around it by faith, and a new
creation will be the result.

I am often asked if I believe in sudden conversion. I
believe in something far more wonderful than sudden
conversion. I believe in sudden regeneration. Conversion is an outward thing; it means merely turning
around: One is faced one way, faced away from God;
he turns around and faces the other way—he faces toward
God. That is conversion. But regeneration goes down
to the very depths of the human heart and spirit. It is a
radical transformation of the innermost man, an impartation of life, and the impartation of a new nature. An
outward conversion, if it is to be real and lasting, must be
the result of an inward regeneration. A man may be
converted a hundred times, but he cannot be born again
but once; for, when one is born again, when God imparts
His Own nature to a man, he stays born again; as John
puts it in 1 Jno. 3:9, "Whosoever is begotten of God is
not doing sin (that is, not making a practice of sin), but
His seed (that is, God's seed, God's Own nature) *abideth
in him:* and he cannot be sinning (that is, making a con-

tinuous practice of sin), because he is begotten of God."
Yes, I believe in sudden regeneration, a sudden, thorough
transformation of the inmost man.

Why do I believe in it? Because this Book teaches it
and because I have seen it over and over again. How
could I doubt it when I had sitting beside me week after
week and year after year on the platform of the Moody
Church in Chicago, as my assistant pastor, a man who, up
to the time he was forty-two years of age was one of the
most desperate and notorious sinners that ever lived, a
man who at the age of nine was a drunkard, and utterly
incorrigible all through his school days, a man who entered the United States Navy at the age of fifteen and
went through the Civil War and learned all the vices of
the navy, and who at the close of the war went into the
regular army and learned all the vices of the army, and
spent a good deal of that time while with the army at
Fort Leavenworth in the guard-house, and was there
elected the leader of a gang of desperados that were confined in the army guard-house at that time, a man who
was ordered out of the city of Omaha by the mayor and
chief of police for almost killing the bully of Omaha in
a fight, a man who rode down the streets of Omaha in a
cab with a revolver in each hand firing the revolvers out
of both windows as he sped down the street, a man who,
in spite of the money he inherited from his father, was
outlawed from the town where he lived in Iowa, but who
came back to that same town one night, went into a Gospel meeting and knelt at the altar and accepted Jesus
Christ and was transformed into the best friend I ever
had in my life, a man I loved as I never loved any other
man, a man of whom if anybody should ask me who was
the most Christlike man I ever met in my life, I would

reply without hesitation, " Rev. William S. Jacoby "—
the dearest man I ever knew; he is now with Christ in
the glory. Yes, I believe in sudden regeneration.

If I did not believe in sudden regeneration, I would
quit preaching, for what would be the use of it all?
What use, for example, of my preaching to such a congregation as I used to preach to every Sunday night in
the Moody Church in Chicago, when that building was
packed of a Sunday night with the motley crowds who
gathered there. There were some of the finest Christians
in Chicago there, there were university students, medical
students, law students, lawyers, doctors, and prominent
business men and earnest Christian men and women were
there, but there were also " jail birds " there, criminals
just out of Joliet State Prison, infidels, outlaws, de-
praved men of pretty much every nation on earth. What
would be the use of preaching to a crowd like that, if it
were not for the regenerating work of the Holy Spirit?
But, believing as I did in the regenerating work of the
Holy Spirit, I always arose to preach with a heart full
of hope and expectation; for I never knew any night
where the Spirit of God, God's Holy Dove, would light.

Take, for example, one specific Sunday night. There
had come into the audience that night, long before the
meeting began, a man so intoxicated that the moment he
was given a seat he went to sleep. He was not turned
out, for we had given our ushers instructions never to
turn out any man no matter how drunk, unless he insisted
on making a disturbance, and, if they were compelled to
turn him out, to follow him out and deal with him and,
if possible, lead him to Christ. This man did not make
a disturbance, except possibly he snored a little. As I
rose to preach that night, I offered a prayer before I

preached, as I usually do; but I offered that night a different prayer from any I ever offered before, and I have never offered the same prayer but once since (and that was when this man asked me to offer it again). I am sure God put it on my lips that night; for I knew nothing about this man. The prayer I offered was this, " Oh God, if there is any man here in Chicago Avenue Church tonight who has run away from New York or from any other Eastern city, and has left his wife and children there to starve, and is drinking himself to death here in Chicago, save that man tonight." Though I had never heard of this man before, when I offered the prayer I had described that man's case exactly. He had not only run away from an Eastern city, but from New York, and he had left his wife and children there to starve, and he was drinking himself to death in Chicago. Just as I offered that prayer he awakened from his slumber, and he heard my words and they sank into his heart. When he left that building he could think of nothing else. As he afterwards described it to me and others, that night he wet his pillow with his tears and God saved him. He got up a regenerated man. Dear man, how well I remember him! I can see his face yet.

That very same night there was a man sitting up in the gallery to my left who was a competent railroad engineer, but who had been blacklisted by every railroad running into Chicago because of his intemperate habits. As I preached that night the Holy Spirit carried my words home to that man's heart and he believed on Jesus Christ and was saved, and born again. As I finished preaching one of my elders stepped up to him and said to him, " Are you saved?" The man replied, " I am." He said, " When were you saved?" He said, " About five min•

utes ago as that man was preaching." The next day that
man went down to the office of the vice-president of the
Chicago and Eastern Illinois Railroad. How an engineer
that was blacklisted by every railroad running into Chicago ever got into the office of the vice-president of the
Chicago and Eastern Illinois Railroad, I do not know;
but he certainly did. He said to the vice-president, " I am
a competent railroad engineer, but I have been blacklisted
by every railroad running into Chicago for getting drunk,
but last night I was converted up in the Moody Church."
The vice-president sprang from the table, went to the
door and locked it and said, " I believe in that sort of
thing, let us pray." And so the vice-president of the
railway and the engineer that was blacklisted by every
railroad running into Chicago, knelt and prayed together.
When they got up from the floor the vice-president said
to him, " Everything I say on this road goes. I will give
you a letter to the foreman of the round-house at Dan-
ville. He will give you an engine."

Oh, yes, I believe in sudden regeneration, and believing
in the regenerating power of the Holy Spirit through the
written Word, knowing that He has power by quickening
the words sown in the human heart to make men and
women all over, I never despair of any man or woman on
earth, and I expect to keep on preaching and teaching the
mighty Word of God in the power of the Holy Ghost as
long as I have strength enough to stand on my feet and
preach. Yes, if God sees fit to put me on a sick bed
before I pass into eternity or before the Lord comes, I
expect to preach Jesus Christ to men there on the sick
bed in the power of the Holy Spirit, and I expect to see
men and women and children born again. Is it any
wonder that I would not give up preaching the Gospel

to be President of the United States or to occupy any throne on earth?

This doctrine of the New Birth is a glorious doctrine. It is true it sweeps away false hopes. It comes to the man who is trusting in his morality and says, " Morality is not enough. YOU MUST BE BORN AGAIN." It comes to the man who is trusting in reform, in turning over a new leaf, and says, " Reform is not enough, no matter how thorough it may be. YOU MUST BE BORN AGAIN." It comes to the man or woman who is trusting in education and culture and says, " Education and culture are not enough—YOU MUST BE BORN AGAIN." It comes to the man or woman who is trusting in his or her amiability of character, in his kindness of heart and generosity in giving, and says, " Amiability of character, kindness of heart and generosity in giving are not enough. YOU MUST BE BORN AGAIN." It comes to the one who is trusting in the externalities of religion, in the fact that he goes to church regularly and has been baptized and united with the Church, and partakes of the Lord's Supper, and regularly reads his Bible and says his prayers; and says, " All the externalities of religion are not enough. YOU MUST BE BORN AGAIN."

Yes, the doctrine of the New Birth sweeps away all the false hopes such as a multitude of you here this morning are building upon, and tells you a better way, the only way. But while it sweeps away false hopes, it brings in a new, a better, a living hope. It comes to each and every one of us and says, " YOU MAY BE BORN AGAIN." It comes to the one who has no taste for the things of God and therefore thinks there is no hope for him, and says. " You may be born again." It comes to the one who is down in sin of one kind or another, the one who is struggling hard but futilely to break away from sin and says, "You may be born again and lose all your love for sin and thus the power of sin be utterly broken." It comes to the one who has wandered so far from God and committed so many sins that he thinks there is no hope for him, that there is nothing to look forward to but an eternal hell, an eternal continuance of the hell he is already in, and that is getting worse every day, the one full of utter and hopeless despair, and says, "YOU MAY BE BORN AGAIN; YOU MAY BE MADE ALL OVER; YOU MAY BECOME A CHILD OF GOD, AND A PARTAKER OF HIS OWN HOLY AND GLORIOUS NATURE." Hallelujah!

Oh, men and women, have you been born again? I do not ask you whether you are church members; I do not ask whether you have been baptized; I do not ask whether you go regularly to the Lord's Supper; I do not ask you whether you are giving as much of your income to the church and to the poor as you should give; I do not ask you whether you go to prayer-meeting regularly, and say your own prayers regularly every day and study your Bible regularly; I ask you, HAVE YOU BEEN BORN AGAIN, have you become a partaker of God's Own nature? If not, you may be today. THE SPIRIT OF GOD IS ABLE AND HE IS READY TO MAKE YOU ALL OVER, TO IMPART TO YOU GOD'S OWN NATURE THROUGH HIS WORD IF YOU WILL ONLY LET HIM DO IT.

IV

HOW TO BE FULLY AND FOREVER
SATISFIED

OUR subject this afternoon is, How to be Fully and Forever Satisfied.

Our Lord Jesus Christ Himself tells us how each one of us can be fully satisfied and satisfied for ever. Turn in your Bibles to John 4: 14: "But whosoever drinketh of the water that I shall give him SHALL NEVER THIRST: but the water that I shall give him shall become in him a well of water springing up into everlasting life." There is a matchless music in these words. I remember how, as a boy, before I had any thought of becoming a Christian myself, I would come back to this verse again and again, and read it over and over. There was to me a fascination in those words that almost no other utterance of our Lord possessed. I did not understand their meaning at all, but they seemed to me like a marvellous strain of music from some far away, heavenly world. But when I came to understand their meaning and to experience for myself the great truth they set forth, there was in them a preciousness that I cannot put into words.

You will recall the circumstances under which the words were spoken. Our Lord Jesus had been taking a long and tiresome journey afoot, covering the entire day. He had started out in the early morning with His disciples, and they had trudged along the whole day through, apparently without anything to eat, and about sunset had reached the outskirts of the village of Sychar. It was formerly thought that the " sixth hour " was noon-time, but it was later discovered that in Ephesus, where John wrote this Gospel, time was reckoned as it is with us today,—from midnight till noon, and from noon till midnight,—and the sixth hour was therefore six o'clock in the afternoon. So "about the sixth hour " was six o'clock in the evening. Our Lord was as truly a real man, as He was " very God of very God;" dusty, tired, hungry, thirsty, He sank upon the well-curb. The disciples went into the town near-by to get something to eat, but apparently He was too tired to accompany them. In a little while, as He sat thus upon the well-curb, looking up the road, He saw a woman of evil character coming toward the well to draw water. Immediately a new thirst took possession of Him—not a thirst for water for His body, but a thirst for the salvation of that outcast woman's soul. As soon as she approached within speaking distance Jesus, seeking an approach to her soul, said: " Give Me to drink;" not so much that He wished water for His thirsty body (though He sorely needed that), as that He wished to win that woman from her sins into the possession of eternal life, which He alone could give. Instead of letting down the jug she carried into the well to draw water, she meanly and contemptuously said: " How is it that Thou, being a Jew, askest drink of me, which am a Samaritan woman?" Our Lord does not notice the insult, but replies: " If thou knewest the gift of God, and who it is that saith to thee, Give Me to drink; thou wouldest have asked of Him, and He would have given thee living water." Immediately the woman said to Him: " Sir. Thou hast nothing to draw with, and the well is deep: from whence then hast Thou that living water?" Pointing down into that well, at which so many generations of men and cattle had slaked their thirst, Jesus replied: "Every one that drinketh of this water shall thirst again."

How true that is of every earthly fountain of satisfaction or joy; no matter how deeply one drinks, he soon thirsts again. For example, drink as deeply as you will of the fountain of wealth, you are not satisfied for long: you soon thirst again. Drink of the fountain of worldly fame or honour or power, how long will you be satisfied? You soon thirst again. Drink as deeply as you will of the fountain of worldly pleasure, you will not be satisfied for long: you soon thrist again. Drink as deeply as you will of the fountain of human knowledge, of the fountain of science, or philosophy, or literature, or at the fountain of music or of art, you soon thirst again. Yes, drink even of that most nearly divine of all human fountains, the fountain of human love, you soon thirst again. Not one of these things fully satisfies, neither do they satisfy for long.

Then our Lord added the wonderful words of our text: "Whosoever shall drink of the water that I shall give him shall never thirst;" or to translate more literally: "shall not thirst forever;" "But the water that I shall give him shall become in him a well of water, springing up into everlasting life." I would that each one of us could sit and ponder those words in silence by ourselves till their full meaning and full force took entire possession of our minds and hearts. DRINK AND KEEP ON DRINKING OF THE WATER THE LORD JESUS GIVES AND YOU WILL BE FULLY AND FOREVER SATISFIED.

But what is the water that our Lord Jesus gives? If you look at the commentaries on John 4: 14, you will find a great many different answers to this question. But the Bible itself answers the question and tells us plainly just what this water is that the Lord Jesus gives. You will find this answer in John 7: 37-39: "Now on the last day, that great day of the feast, Jesus stood and cried, saying, If any man thirst, let him come unto Me and drink. He that believeth on Me, as the Scripture hath said, out of his belly shall flow rivers of living water. (*But this spake He of the Spirit,* which they that believe on Him were to receive. For the Spirit was not yet given: because Jesus was not yet glorified)."

Here we are told that THE WATER WHICH JESUS CHRIST GIVES IS THE HOLY SPIRIT, Whom He gives to those who believe on Him and who ask Him for the Gift (cf. vs. 10). Any one who really receives the Holy Spirit as an indwelling presence will be fully and forever satisfied, and that is the only possible way to be fully and forever satisfied.

It is a great thing to have your source of joy within yourself; to have your joy, not in your environment, nor in your circumstances, nor in your possessions, but to have your fountain of joy within your own heart. If our joy is in our environment or in our possessions we cannot by any possibility be always happy; for sometimes our environment is just what we would have it to be, and sometimes it is just what we would not have it to be. When our environment is pleasant, then we are happy, but when it is unpleasant we are miserable. If our joy is in our possessions,—that is, in our possessions outside of ourselves—we cannot by any possibility be always happy, for sometimes we have them, and sometimes we lose them. When we have them we are happy, but when they are gone we are utterly miserable. We are happy when we are rich, but we are miserable when we are poor. We are happy when we are well, but we are miserable when we are sick. We are happy when men speak well of us, but we are miserable when they speak evil of us. We are happy when we have our friends with us, but plunged into the depths of sorrow and despair when they are taken from us by death.

But if our source of joy is in our own hearts, a fountain springing up within us, then we are entirely independent of our surroundings, our circumstances, our possessions or lack of possessions. We are joyful when we are rich and equally joyful when we are poor; we are joyful when things go just right, and equally joyful when they go " dead wrong;" we are joyful when we are well, but equally joyful when we are sick; we are joyful when men speak well of us, but equally joyful when they speak all manner of evil against us; we are joyful when we have our friends with us, but equally joyful when the dearest friend we have on earth is taken from us; indeed, the joy of the indwelling Spirit of God seems oftentimes to well up with even greater power in the moments of deepest bereavement. In that dark hour that comes, sooner or later, to every one of us, when for the last time we look into the face of some dearly loved one lying cold and still in death, what possible comfort is there in anything that this world can give? Is there any surcease for our sorrow in such an hour to be gained by going to the theatre, the opera, the card-party, the dance? No, those things would only add to our sorrow. We do not think of going to them at such an hour. But from this fountain within us, which the indwelling Spirit has become, gushes up at such a time as that " joy unspeakable and full of glory."

How well I remember such an experience in a time of apparently overwhelming sorrow that came to my wife and to me years ago. We had a lovely daughter, about nine years of age, a most winsome child. One Saturday afternoon Mr. Jacoby, the redeemed man of whom I spoke to you yesterday, came to our house, as he did every Saturday afternoon, to take the children with him out to Lincoln Park. When they returned that evening about six o'clock, our little Elizabeth said: "I don't think I'll eat any supper tonight; I don't feel real well." We thought little of it, considering it simply a bilious attack. But the next morning when she came down to breakfast she said: "I don't think I'll go to church this morning; my head aches." We still thought it was simply a bilious attack. But Monday morning, when she came to the breakfast-table, she said: "I don't feel real well yet; I don't think I'd better go to school today." It seemed rather long for a bilious attack to stay with a child, and yet it seemed nothing serious. She was around the house all day, not feeling really well, but apparently not very sick. Tuesday morning, when she arose, she said: "I am well today and I'm going to school." But she added: "I have a strange feeling in my throat!" Her mother looked into her throat and saw the tell-tale white patch, and, of course, we sent for a physician at once. When he came and had carefully examined the child he said: "There is nothing to be anxious about. It is not diphtheria; it is only tonsilitis. But I will keep a close watch." The next morning he came again and gave her another examination, and then said: "Well, it is diphtheria, but not a serious case at all. There is nothing to be alarmed about."

The other children were sent away from home, so that

they might not be exposed. Our Elizabeth seemed to be better all that day. That night I slept down-stairs to avoid exposing others whom I might have to meet during the following day, and her mother stayed up-stairs with the little child. The next morning, long before daylight, her mother ran to the top of the stairs, calling: " Archie, come up, quick! " I rushed up-stairs and saw Elizabeth choking. I ran at once for the physician. He came back with me; but Elizabeth was apparently very much better. The choking had all passed away; indeed, she seemed well on the road to recovery. The doctor said: " For some reason or other I don't feel like administering anti-toxin; but keep a close watch on her, and if she gets any worse telephone me at the Medical College and I will leave my classes and come at once." But she seemed to rapidly grow better rather than worse; indeed, she said to her mother: " Mother, I am well; I want to get up and dress." In the meantime, a trained nurse had come, and her mother came down-stairs to talk with me. We were very happy in the thought that our little girl had been spared to us, and I had written letters to Mr. Moody and other friends saying how the crisis was past and Elizabeth was well on the road to recovery.

Suddenly, right in the midst of our talk with one another, the nurse ran to the top of the stairs and called: " Come up, quick! " We rushed up-stairs. Elizabeth's eyes were closed. She was breathing rapidly, not chok-ing, but the little heart was giving out. There was no time to send for the doctor. I dropped on my knees to pray. I had hardly time to begin when the spirit of our little one had taken its flight from the mortal body. It was so sudden, so unexpected, it was almost crushing. The health officers came in and ordered that we should bury the body at once. Of course, no one was allowed to come to the funeral. We had to have the service all alone, with the exception of the presence of Mr. Jacoby, who insisted on coming and accompanying us to the grave. Even her brother and little sisters could only stand across the street and look at the house where lay the body of their sister, whom they would never see again until the resurrection. We carried the little body to the cemetery. It was raining pitilessly, and as the little body was lowered into the grave and the rain poured upon the box that contained the casket, my wife turned to me and said: " Archie, I am so glad that Elizabeth is not in that box! "

When we returned home the health officers demanded, very wisely, that after being fumigated we should leave the house to them and go to a strange hotel for the night. All that night there was the most prolonged thunder-storm, except one, that I ever passed through. It seemed to be one unceasing flash of lightning and crash of thunder, and we could not sleep.

The next morning, as I went, thoroughly worn out, to the Bible Institute to meet my classes, as I passed around the corner of Chestnut Street and La Salle Avenue, I could contain my grief no longer. There was no one on the street, and I cried aloud: " Oh, Elizabeth! Elizabeth! " And just then this fountain that I had in my heart broke forth with such power as I think I had never experienced before, and it was the most joyful moment that I had ever known in my life!

Oh, how wonderful is the joy of the Holy Ghost! It is an unspeakably glorious thing to have your joy, not in things without you, not even in your most dearly loved friends, but to have within you a fountain ever springing

up, springing up, springing up, always springing up, three
hundred and sixty-five days in every year, springing up
under all circumstances into everlasting life.

It is also a great thing that you can have a fountain
that you can take with you wherever you go. A good
many years ago I was walking along the Winchester Road
in Northfield with George Needham, the celebrated evangelist. We went over the state line into New Hampshire.
On our return, when we had reached a place about five
minutes north of where the Auditorium now stands, we
passed by a hill. Mr. Needham said to me: "Torrey, I
believe that if we go up to the top of that hill we will
get a fine view." So up to the top of the hill we went,
and it was a wonderful view! At our feet lay the Northfield Seminary grounds in all their beauty. Then across
the road, the meadows leading down to the Connecticut
River, that ran like a broad silver band between the
gentle slopes of green on both sides of the river. Then
one tier of hills and then another a little higher, then
another, then another—five, six, seven tiers, ending in
the Green Mountains in the distance, and all bathed in
the golden light of the setting sun! It was a scene of
marvellous beauty. I turned to Mr. Needham and said:
"I am going to buy this hill and build a house right
where we are standing!" So the next day I went to the
farmer who owned the land; he named his price, and I
paid it. The following spring I began to build my house.
My friends who drove along the foot of the hill would
call to me, and when I would go down would say: "What
are you building 'way up there for?" I would reply:
"Because I wish to see out." "But," they said, "you
will have no water up there!"

That is where they were mistaken; for before a spade

was put into the ground to dig the foundations, in walking over the place with the farmer from whom I had purchased it, I noticed a little depression in the ground, perhaps fifty or seventy-five feet from where I had intended to build the house. I said to the farmer: " I think if we should dig there we would strike water." He replied: " I don't know; it looks as if you might." I sent for a well-digger. He dug a hole four or five feet across and eight feet deep—and the water came bubbling in. There were soon five feet of water in that eight-foot-deep well, and such water! Clear as crystal—so clear that when you looked into the well, even when there were five feet of water in it, it looked sometimes as if there were none, the water was so clear and transparent. And water soft and cold and pure and never-failing! We had many dry seasons after that and many another well ran dry; but not our well, up on the hillside. There was always plenty of water in that spring and many would come there to drink.

But there was one grave trouble with that well—a fatal fault—I could not take it with me when the call came for me to go elsewhere. During the Spanish-American War I was with the soldiers at Chickamauga Park, and we had a prolonged drought; for weeks and weeks no rain; and with sixty thousand troops marching and counter-marching, and artillery wagons running across the field, the dust filled the air day and night—dust thirty feet high! We ate dust, we drank dust we slept dust, and we drempt dust! And no water anywhere fit to drink. There was a well to which the officers of Major-General Brooks' command had access, and it looked good and tasted good, but drink it and in a short time you would be flat on your back. And oh, how

thirsty I got, and how often I would think of that well
of mine up on the hill at Northfield! But it did me no
good, for it was many hundreds of miles away.

Then the call came for me to go to China, and while
in China we decided to visit Canton. Cholera was raging
in Canton at the time. People were fleeing from the
city in fright. When we boarded the boat at Hong-Kong
to go up to Canton, they said to us: "Be sure and drink
no water on the boat. A member of the French Legation
went up last week and drank water on that boat. He was
at breakfast with his family, but died with cholera before
lunch." I remembered the warning on the way up, but
after a few days in Canton, when we were going back
on the steamer, as I sat down to dinner I read on the
menu card: "Corned beef and cabbage." That looked
good to an American who had been eating all kinds of
foreign concoctions. Without thinking of what it would
do for me, I ordered corned beef and cabbage. But I
soon found what it would do for me! In the evening I
began to get very thirsty. I was about to start for the
water-tank when I remembered the warning: "Be sure
and drink no water on the boat. A member of the French
Legation went up last week and drank some water on
the boat. He was with his family at breakfast and died
with cholera before lunch!" So I drank some of the
various soft-drink concoctions as long as I dared, and
then lay all night suffering from thirst and thinking of
the well on the hillside at Northfield, so many thousands
of miles away. But I had another Well that I had
brought with me, and while my body thirsted, my soul
was satisfied: the Holy Spirit within was springing up,
springing up, springing up, into everlasting life and joy!

Please note another thing: when one has this fountain

of satisfaction and joy within him, he is entirely independent of the world's sources of joy. What does he care for the dance, or the card-party, or the theatre, or any other kind of earthly satisfaction? Who would go to an old green, slimy pool to drink when he had right at hand a clear crystal spring? Oh, the world with its allurements has no power over the one who has this fountain within!

I often think there is little use in telling young Christians: You must not dance; you must not play cards; you must not go to the theatre; you must not do this, that and the other thing. There is a far better way: Get them to receive the Holy Spirit, and let Him have full right of way within, and they will have no desire for such things—they will stay away from the theatre and the dance, and the rest, not merely because they *ought,* but because they will not desire to go. Who that knows of a clear, crystal spring will sneak off to some green, slimy pool to drink?

When Mr. Moody was holding meetings in Philadelphia, a lady came to him one day at the close of one of his meetings and said: " Mr. Moody, I don't like you! " " Why? " he asked. " Because you are so narrow." " I didn't think I was narrow," Mr. Moody replied; " why do you think I am narrow? " " Because you don't believe in the dance, you don't believe in cards, you don't believe in the theatre, you don't believe in anything nice! " " Let me tell you something," he said, " I go to the theatre whenever I want to." " What! " she exclaimed, " you go to the theatre whenever you want to? Oh, I do like you, Mr. Moody! You are much broader than I thought." " Yes," he replied, " I go to the theatre whenever I want to, I DON'T WANT TO! "

Some days later another lady came to him and said: "Mr. Moody, I did not understand what you meant when you said you went to the theatre whenever you wanted to, but I understand now. I was converted in your meetings and a few days ago, after my conversion, my husband asked me to go to the theatre with him. I did not care to go, but went to please him. We had hardly taken our seats when the curtain rose and just a little while after the curtain rose something was said on the stage that grated on this new life that I had in my heart. I turned to my husband and whispered: 'Husband, I can't stand this!' He whispered back: 'Stay through this play and I will never ask you to come again.' I straightened up and the play went on for a little while longer, and again something was said or done on the stage that grated on this new life in my heart. Again I turned to my husband and whispered: 'Husband, I really can't stand this; I must go!' My husband whispered back: 'Don't make a scene. Stay through this play and I'll never ask you to come again.' Again I straightened up and tried to endure it. But soon something else was said or done that jarred upon this new life that I had in my heart, and I turned to my husband and said: 'Husband, I really can't stand it any longer!' He whispered back: 'Don't make a fool of yourself!' I replied: 'Husband, I have been making a fool of myself for thirty years, and I am not going to make a fool of myself any longer!' And I got up and left."

Oh, if you have this fountain within, you will not want these things. The pure crystal spring of the Holy Spirit in the heart will make it impossible for you to seek to slake your thirst at the green, slimy pools of this world's pleasures.

But someone will ask: Why is it, then, that so many Christians do run after these things? The answer is very simple: It is either because they never have really received the Holy Spirit as an indwelling fountain of life and joy and satisfaction, which is doubtless true of many professing Christians; or else the fountain has become choked. You know it is quite possible to choke a fountain.

I was born in the city and brought up in the city. Occasionally, in the summer, our family would take a vacation in the country. But in the heart of the great city was where we lived. When I became ten years of age I was thoroughly tired of the city, as any healthy boy would be. My two brothers, who were both older than I, were also tired of the city, and we went to our father and said: "Father, buy a home in the country." He was born in the country and was, I suspect, more tired of the city than we were, and, though he was only forty-three, he made up his mind that he would retire from business and would buy a home in the country. He went to Geneva, N. Y., about twenty miles from where he was born. Oftentimes, as a young man, he had noticed a beautiful place on Seneca Lake where he thought he would like to live when he had money enough to make it possible. It was just outside Geneva, across the lake, the grounds running down to the lake. But, on reaching Geneva, he found that the owner did not wish to sell the place. He went to an old friend, an elder in the Presbyterian Church, Captain Joe Lewis, and said: "Joe, I came out here to buy the Swan place but they don't wish to sell it. I am greatly disappointed!" "Reuben," he replied, "I think I know a place that would suit you—the Colonel Sherrill place. The colonel was killed in the war, and his widow wishes to sell the place." He took my father out, and they soon agreed upon the terms and my father bought the place.

Geneva is a beautiful city lying at the foot of Seneca Lake, one of the most beautiful sheets of water in the world, forty-two miles long and from two to five miles wide. The man who had originally built the place had spent a great deal of money upon it. It was half a mile from the lake and part of the city lay between the place and the lake. But the man wished to see up the lake. So he had three hundred teams to work for many weeks building an artificial hill, so that they could see over the lake and up the lake twenty miles. Then he laid out his lawns and gardens and sent to different parts of this country and, I think, also to England, to get large trees to set out. But when the trees were set out and the house and barns and stables built, and the orchards planted, though he could see twenty miles up the lake the man was not satisfied, because of the water supply. There was a good well, but it was a long ways from the house, and he wished to have a well near at hand where he could pump water through the house. He sent for well diggers and set them to digging a well not very far from the house. They dug and dug and dug; it seemed as if they never would strike water. But one day they struck water and struck altogether too much. They struck a " gusher " and the water came pouring in until they were afraid it would undermine the foundations of the house. He sent for the fire department; they pumped the well out, and while still pumping they lowered a man in a basket down into the well with a rag carpet in his hand. He found the great orifice where the water was pouring in and shoving the rag carpet in stopped the flow of water. Then they piled in rocks on top of it, and the well was perfectly safe. But it was also perfectly useless.

One day, standing by that expensive hole, the man said to himself: " I put a lot of money into that hole and I am going to have that water!" They took out the rocks that had been piled in, then curbed the well up with stone from the bottom to the top; and then he sent for the fire department again. Again they lowered the man into the well. In one hand he held a cord with which to pull a bell to signal them when he got hold of the carpet. He took hold of the carpet with one hand and with the other rang the signal, and they pulled him up, dragging the carpet with him. And the water poured in again, but now it was perfectly safe.

For years we drank of that well, and wonderful water it was. But in the course of time my father and mother died, and the place passed into other hands. I never revisited the place after my father's funeral for twenty-two years; I did not want to see it. But one time I had to pass through Geneva to go to Cornell University to speak at a meeting there. On returning through the place I thought I would get off and visit the old place. The station of the Lehigh Valley railroad was right on our old place, about a quarter of a mile back from where the house had stood. A street-car line passed right over the spot where the house had been located. I got off and looked to see if I could find anything that reminded me of the old home. The house had been taken down, brick by brick and stone by stone. Many of the finest trees had been cut down. The lawns and gardens and orchards were now laid out in city lots. I thought at first I was to find nothing that belonged to the old home. But passing by a house I noticed a well right in front of the front porch. I thought to myself: " What a strange place to have a well, right in the front yard and in front of the porch;" and then it occurred to me that it was the old well! Leaving the old home place, I went down town. The Presbyterian minister met me on the street. " Oh," he said, " have you been up to the old place? " I replied: " I have." He said: " You didn't find anything of the old place left, did you? " " Yes," I said, " just one thing—the old well. But what a strange place for a well—right in front of your front porch! I should think they would fill it up." He replied: " They will never fill that well up—it's the best water in Geneva! " Do you see the point?—the best water in Geneva! and yet it had been plugged up for a long time with an old rag! If you have ever received the Holy Spirit as an indwelling source of joy, you have had in your heart, not " the best water there is in Geneva," but the best water there is in the universe. And in many of you the well is plugged up by some old rag of sin or worldly conformity. Let's pull out the old rags today! What do you say?

When I was holding meetings in Melbourne, Australia, I used this illustration one day at a meeting for business and professional men in the town hall. There was a Church of England clergyman in my audience who had known the joy of the Holy Spirit in his earlier life in England, but in coming out to Australia the fountain had become choked. As he heard me that day a great unrest came into his heart; he longed for the old joy. He spent the whole afternoon at the Cathedral in prayer (the Cathedral was kept open all day for prayer). But when night came on he had not got the old rag out yet. He called upon Father Kent, a godly Anglican clergyman, and told him of his trouble, and Father Kent helped him to get the old rag out, and he was filled with even greater joy than he had known before. He came to me the next day and told me of the experience. When we went to Geelong to hold meetings there, this man, whose parish was fifteen miles from Geelong, brought a wagon-load of people down every night to the meeting and took them back again after the meeting was over. He was the most useful worker we had in Geelong.

Oh, if you have ever known this joy and have lost it, find out today what it is that stops the well and have it out, and you will know not only as great but very likely a greater joy than you knew before.

When I was holding meetings in Bristol, England, in the Coulston Hall, I spoke one afternoon on this same subject. At the close, as I stepped into my carriage to go to my hotel, another Anglican clergyman came up and said: "I am going to ride to the hotel with you," and stepped into the carriage with me. We had not gone far when he said: "I once knew this joy of which you have been speaking today, but the fountain is now plugged, and I know what plugs it—it is a plug of tobacco! I am going to give it up today."

What is it that stops the fountain in your heart? Do you know? If so, put it away today. But perhaps you do not know what it is. You know you once had that joy and you know you have lost it. Well, you can know. Ask God to show you what it is that stops the fountain and promise Him that if He will show you what it is, you will give it up. He will show you if you are really sincere.

But perhaps some of you never knew the joy of the Holy Spirit. You can know that wondrous joy today. The Lord Jesus stands here today, all unseen, but nevertheless here, holding out the golden goblet that contains the living water, and saying: " Whosoever drinketh of the water that I shall give him shall never thirst; but the water that I shall give him shall become in him a well of water, springing up into everlasting life." Will you drink?

Further back in the chapter the Lord Jesus says (in vs. 10) : " If thou knowest the gift of God and who it is that saith to thee, Give me to drink, thou wouldest have *asked of Him*, and he would have given thee living water." Just ask of the Lord Jesus, but be sure, when you ask, that you really mean it, and that you really long for the Holy Spirit at any price, and that your will is fully surrendered to God, for He gives the Holy Spirit " to them that obey Him " (Acts 5 : 32).

V

THE BAPTISM WITH THE HOLY SPIRIT:
WHAT IT IS AND WHAT IT DOES

THE address of this afternoon, and the addresses of the days immediately to follow, are the outcome of an experience, and that experience was the outcome of a study of the Word of God. After I had been a Christian for some years, and after I had been in the ministry for some years, my attention was strongly attracted to certain phrases found in the Gospels and in the Acts of the Apostles, and in the Epistles, such as "baptized with the Holy Spirit," "filled with the Spirit," "the Holy Spirit fell upon them," "the gift of the Holy Spirit," "endued with power from on high," and other closely allied phrases. As I studied these various phrases in their context, it became clear to me that they all stood for essentially the same experience; and it also became clear to me that God had provided for each child of His in this present dispensation that they should be this "baptized with the Spirit," or, "filled with the Spirit."

As I studied the subject still further, I became convinced that they described an experience which I did not myself possess, and I went to work to secure for myself the experience thus described. I sought earnestly that I might "be baptized with the Holy Spirit." I went at it very ignorantly. I have often wondered if anyone ever went at it any more ignorantly than I did. But while I was ignorant, I was thoroughly sincere and in earnest, and God met me, as He always meets the sincere and earnest soul, no matter how ignorant he may be; and God gave me what I sought, I was "baptized with the Holy Spirit." And the result was a transformed Christian life and a transformed ministry.

Then I began to tell others of what I had found in the Word of God, first in very small circles, then in larger circles, then in much wider circles, and at last it was my privilege to tell it literally around the globe. I have often thought, in connection with my own experience, of our Lord's own promise to the apostles, found in Acts 1:8. "But ye shall receive power, after that the Holy Ghost is come upon you: and ye shall be witnesses unto me both in Jerusalem and in all Judea, and in Samaria, *and unto the uttermost part of the earth*"; for it has been my privilege to declare the truth in the very remotest inhabited spot there is on this globe from the place where I myself was "baptized with the Holy Spirit."

You will find the substance of all I have to say this afternoon, in three verses in the Bible, Acts 1:4, 5, 8: "And being assembled together with them (He) commanded them that they should not depart from Jerusalem, but wait for the promise of the Father, which, saith He, ye have heard of Me. For John truly baptized with water; but *ye shall be baptized with the Holy Ghost* not many days hence. . . . But *ye shall receive power, after that the Holy Ghost is come upon you:* and *ye shall be witnesses unto me* both in Jerusalem, and in all Judea, and in Samaria, and unto the uttermost part of the earth." What I wish you to notice particularly just now, in these verses, is these words, "BAPTIZED WITH THE

HOLY GHOST." What a peculiar expression it is! What does it mean? We all know what it means to be baptized with water: we have seen people thus baptized. But " baptized with the Holy Ghost," what does it mean?

What I have to say on the general subject of the Baptism with the Holy Spirit, will come under five heads:

First: What the Baptism with the Holy Spirit Is.

Second: What the Results of the Baptism with the Holy Spirit Are.

Third: The Necessity of the Baptism with the Holy Spirit, or, Who Needs the Baptism with the Holy Spirit.

Fourth: The Possibility of the Baptism with the Holy Spirit, or Who Can Be Baptized with the Holy Spirit.

Fifth: How the Baptism with the Holy Spirit Is to Be Obtained.

I. WHAT IS THE BAPTISM WITH THE HOLY SPIRIT?

The first question, then, that we should consider is, " What is the Baptism with the Holy Spirit? " The Bible makes this very plain, if we study the various passages that speak of the subject, and study them in their context.

1. In the first place, the *Baptism with the Holy Spirit is a definite experience of which one may know whether he has received it or not.* This is clear from Acts 1:4, 5: " And being assembled together with them (He) commanded them that they should not depart from Jerusalem, but *wait for the promise of the Father,* which, saith He, ye have heard from Me. For John indeed baptized with water; but *ye shall be baptized with the Holy Ghost not many days hence.*" It is clear as day from these verses that the Baptism with the Holy Ghost is a definite experience of which a man may know whether he has received it or not, for if not, how could the disciples possibly know when the days of *waiting* were over and the days to begin their ministry had begun?

The same thing is clear from Acts 19:2 also: "He said unto them, Have ye received the Holy Ghost since ye believed?" or, as it is in the Revised Version, "Did ye receive the Holy Ghost *when ye believed?*" "And they said unto him, No, we did not so much as hear whether the Holy Ghost was given." Paul had come down to the City of Ephesus, and had found there a small group of disciples, twelve in number. There was something about these twelve disciples that did not altogether satisfy Paul. We are not told just what it was. It may have been that there was not that abounding joyfulness about them that one expects to find in Spirit-filled Christians. It may be that Paul was troubled by the fact that there were only twelve of them, thinking that if they were Spirit-filled, there would certainly have been more than twelve of them by this time. Whatever it was that disturbed Paul, he went right to the root of the difficulty at once by putting to them the question that we have just read, "*Did ye receive the Holy Ghost* when ye believed?" Evidently Paul expected a definite "Yes," or a definite "No" in answer to that question. In point of fact he got a definite "No." They said "No, we did not so much as hear whether the Holy Ghost was given." They did not say what our Authorized Version makes them say: "We have not so much as heard whether there be any Holy Ghost." I suppose there are Christians today who are as ignorant as that, they do not even know that there is such a person as the Holy Spirit, but these disciples knew that there was a Holy Spirit. They knew, furthermore, that there was a definite promise of the baptism with the Holy Ghost, but they did not know that that promise had as yet been fulfilled. Paul assured them that it had, and saw to it at once, even before that meeting broke up, that they all took the steps whereby they were all definitely and immediately baptized with the Holy Ghost right then and there without any " tarrying meetings " or anything of that sort.

There is much talk in these days about the Baptism with the Holy Spirit, and much prayer for the Baptism with the Holy Spirit that is altogether vague and indefinite. You will go to a meeting and men will stand up and pray that they may be baptized with the Holy Ghost, but oftentimes, if after the meeting is over you should go to them and ask, " Did you get what you asked? Were you baptized with the Holy Ghost? " there is quite a strong probability that they would hesitate, and even stammer, and say, " Well, well, *I hope so.*" But there is none of that indefiniteness in the Bible. The Bible is the most definite book that was ever written. That is one of the reasons why I love it. The Bible is definite about salvation; so definite that if a man is saved, *and knows his Bible,* and you put to him the question, " Are you saved," he will reply, in all humility and yet with equal confidence, " Yes, God in His infinite mercy and condescension has saved even me." The Bible is just as definite about the Baptism with the Holy Spirit; so definite that if a man has been " baptized with the Holy Spirit," *and knows his Bible,* and you put to him the question, " Have you been baptized with the Holy Spirit? " he will reply, in all humility and yet with equal confidence and positiveness, " Yes, God in His infinite mercy and condescension has seen fit to baptize even me with His Holy Spirit."

Of course, it is quite possible that a man may be a saved man and yet, by reason of his ignorance of the Bible, not have assurance of salvation, *i. e.*, he may not *know* that he is saved. We have all met many such men and women. But it is his privilege to know (1 Jno. 5:13). And so it is also quite possible that a man may have been "baptized with the Holy Ghost" and yet, *through ignorance of the Bible,* not know the name of the experience which he has received. I have met such men and women as that. I remember a man who came to me once at an "International Christian Workers' Convention" at Washington, D. C. He was a well-known man—a man known all over the country; a man that I presume every one of you would know at least by name if I should mention it. At the close of an address that I gave on "The Baptism with the Holy Spirit," this man came to me and said, "Is that what you call it, the Baptism with the Holy Spirit? I never heard the name before, but I have received what you have been talking about, and I can tell you just where I received it." But, while this is all true, it is possible for us to know whether or not we have been baptized with the Holy Spirit. THE BAPTISM WITH THE HOLY SPIRIT IS A DEFINITE EXPERIENCE OF WHICH ONE MAY KNOW WHETHER HE HAS RECEIVED IT OR NOT.

2. In the second place, *the Baptism with the Holy Spirit is a work of the Holy Spirit distinct from and additional to His regenerating work.* In other words, it is one thing to be born again by the Holy Spirit, and quite another thing to be baptized with the Holy Spirit. This is very evident from Acts 1:5: "Ye shall be baptized with the Holy Ghost, not many days hence." It is evident from these words that the apostles had not as yet been baptized with the Holy Spirit, they were to be "not many days hence." But *the men to whom our Lord Jesus Christ spoke these words were already regenerate men.* We know that they were regenerate men because our Lord Jesus Christ Himself had pronounced them to be regenerate men. In John 15:3, our Lord had said sometime before to these very same men, "*Already ye are clean because of the word* which I have spoken unto you." Now, what does "clean because of the word" mean? Turn to 1 Peter 1:23, and you will get your answer: "Having been *begotten again,* not of corruptible seed, but of incorruptible, *through the word of God,* which liveth and abideth." It is evident from these words that "clean through the Word" (or "because of the Word," as the Revised Version reads) means "begotten again," or born again, "through the Word." So *these men were already born again,* but they were not as yet baptized with the Holy Spirit. They were to be "baptized with the Holy Spirit" not many days hence.

The same thing is evident from Acts 8:12-16. In verse 12 we are told that "when *they believed* Philip preaching *the good tidings concerning* the kingdom of God, and *the name of Jesus Christ,* they *were baptized,* both men and women." Now certainly, in that large company of baptized believers, who had "believed Philip preaching good tidings concerning the kingdom of God, and the name of Jesus Christ," and who "*had been baptized into the name of the Lord Jesus*" (v. 16), there were at least some who were regenerate men and women. Whatever may be the correct mode of baptism, by sprinkling, immersion, or pouring, these disciples had, beyond question, been baptized in the right way, for Philip, an officially appointed officer in the church, had administered the baptism, and as I have said, it is clear that some, at least, of this company of properly baptized believers were regenerate men. But when we come down to verses 15 and 16, we read, " Peter and John, when they were come down, *prayed for them that they might receive the Holy Ghost: for as yet He was fallen upon none of them:* only they were *baptized* into the name of the *Lord Jesus."* So we see clearly that these regenerate men had not been baptized with the Holy Ghost, though they had been properly " baptized into the name of the Lord Jesus." *They were regenerate men* but *they were not baptized with the Holy Spirit.*

So it IS AS CLEAR AS LANGUAGE CAN POSSIBLY MAKE IT, THAT IT IS ONE THING TO BE BORN AGAIN AND SOME-THING FURTHER, SOMETHING ADDITIONAL, TO BE BAPTIZED WITH THE HOLY SPIRIT. It is clear and undeniable, therefore, that one may be a regenerate man and yet not as yet have received the baptism with the Holy Spirit. Let us bow to the clear teaching of the Word of God even if it does not agree with our preconceived theories.

Now, if a man is regenerate, he is saved. This is not a question of salvation at all. If he should die he would go to heaven. *But though he is saved he is not yet fitted for God's service.* He has not as yet all that he might have, and ought to have.

Let me make it clear, still further, that *every believer has the Holy Spirit in some sense; that the Holy Spirit dwells in every one that is born again.* This appears clearly from Romans 8:9, as well as from many other passages of Scripture. Let me read Romans 8:9 to you: " But if any man have not the Spirit of Christ, he is none of His." Now the words " the Spirit of Christ " in this verse do not mean a Christlike spirit. The words

are a name for the Holy Spirit; that is clear from the
context. And what we are told here is that if any man
hath not the Holy Spirit (Who is here called the Spirit
of Christ), he is none of His. *So it is clear that every
regenerate man has the Holy Spirit.* But in many a
believer the Holy Spirit dwells away back in some hidden
sanctuary of his person, away back of conscious experience. So, just as it is one thing to have a guest in your
house living in some remote corner of the house where
you scarcely know that he is there, and quite another
thing to have that guest taking entire possession of the
house, just so it is one thing to have the Holy Spirit
dwelling away back of consciousness in some hidden
sanctuary of our being, and quite another thing to have
that Holy Spirit taking entire possession of the house.
In other words, it is one thing to have the Holy Spirit
merely dwelling in us but we not conscious of His
dwelling, and *quite another* thing to be filled, or baptized,
with the Holy Spirit. So we may put it with perfect
accuracy in this way: Every regenerate person has the
Holy Spirit, but not every regenerate person has what
the Bible calls "*the gift of the Holy Spirit,*" or "*The
baptism with the Holy Spirit,*" or "the Promise of the
Father."

Let me say, still further, that *one may be baptized with
the Holy Spirit at the very time he is born again.* That
is exactly what occurred in the case of the household of
Cornelius. Cornelius and his household and friends were
listening to the first gospel sermon they had ever heard
in their lives, and Peter had come to the climax of his
sermon, in Acts 10:43, where he says: "To Him (*i. e.,*
to the Lord Jesus) bear all the prophets witness, that
through His name everyone that believeth on Him shall

receive remission of sins," and no sooner had Peter said it than they all believed on the Lord Jesus and were born again, and right then and there, before Peter could finish his sermon, we read, "*While Peter yet spake these words,* the Holy Spirit fell on all them that heard the Word. And they of the circumcision that believed were amazed, as many as came with Peter, because that on the Gentiles also *was poured out the gift of the Holy Spirit.* For they heard them speak with tongues and magnify God." So we see that they were baptized with the Holy Spirit the very moment that they believed and were born again. Now in a normal order of the Church, I believe that this would be the common experience; but alas! the Church is not in a normal order today. A very large portion of the Church of Jesus Christ today is exactly where the believers in Samaria were before Peter and John came down *and " prayed for them that they might receive the Holy Spirit"* because "as yet He was fallen upon not one of them." They are just where the twelve disciples in Ephesus were before Paul visited Ephesus; baptized with the baptism of repentance, *forgiven and saved,* but *not yet baptized with the Holy Spirit.*

The Baptism with the Holy Spirit is every believer's privilege and birthright, through the crucified, risen and ascended Saviour. Jesus Christ, when He ascended up on high, prayed for His Church (Jno. 14: 15-17), that is, for the whole body of believers, and received for them, as we are told in Acts 2: 33, "the promise of the Holy Spirit" and poured forth the Holy Spirit upon His Church as a body, but many members of the true Church, that is, many saved men and women, have not claimed for themselves their birthright; and so, while the baptism with the Holy Spirit is theirs, *i. e.,* it belongs to them, *they do not as yet have the baptism with the Holy Spirit in experimental possession.*

We may say, further still, that it is by "the Baptism with the Holy Spirit" that the individual believer, as we are told in 1 Cor. 12:13, is "baptized into the Body" of Jesus Christ *as a living, active, efficient member of that Body;* but many believers have not claimed this "Baptism with the Holy Spirit," and therefore are not possessors of those gifts (see 1 Cor. 12:4-11) that qualify them to be members of the Body in the sense in which Paul is describing the Body in the twelfth chapter of First Corinthians. They are potentially baptized with the Holy Spirit but not experimentally so baptized, but they may be at once.

In any event the passages that we have read, and many others that we might read, make it clear to any one whose mind is subject to the Word of God, and who therefore simply desires to know what the Word of God teaches and is not the slave of a theory, that one may be born again and yet not be baptized with the Holy Spirit. Furthermore, from our own observation and experience today, we must all know that *if the baptism with the Holy Spirit means anything definite, as it certainly did in Bible days, as set forth in both the Acts and in the Epistles,* then there are many people in the Church today who we have a right to believe are born again and thus saved, who are not as yet baptized with the Holy Spirit.

3. In the third place, *the baptism with the Holy Spirit is a work of the Holy Spirit always connected with and primarily for the purpose of testimony and service.* This is evident from the passage where our Lord Jesus made the original promise of the baptism with the Holy Spirit, Acts 1:8: "But ye *shall receive power,* when the Holy

Spirit is come upon you: and *ye shall be my witnesses* both in Jerusalem, and in all Judea, and in Samaria, and unto the uttermost part of the earth." The same thing is evident from the twelfth chapter of First Corinthians, where the whole subject of the Baptism with the Holy Spirit is treated at length and in detail. We will not take time to read the passage now, although we shall have occasion to read much of it later. *There is not one single passage in the Bible, either in the Old Testament or the New Testament, where the Baptism with the Holy Spirit is spoken of, where it is not connected with testimony or service.* I made this statement some years ago in speaking to a large class of theological students. At the close of the lecture two students came up to me and said, " Did we understand you to say, Mr. Torrey, that there was not a single passage in the Bible, where the Baptism with the Holy Spirit is mentioned, where it is not connected with testimony or service?" "Yes," I replied, "that is exactly what I said." "Well," they said, "we doubt it." I replied, "You have a perfect right to doubt it, but now go and search your Bible and bring me, if you can, one single passage in the Bible where the Baptism with the Holy Spirit is definitely mentioned or referred to, where it is not connected with testimony or service." They went to work to search for the passage. I think they must be searching for it yet, for they have never brought it to me; and they never will, for it is not to be found anywhere in the Bible. I have gone through my Bible on this subject, time and time again since I made that remark to those students, and without the slightest fear of successful contradiction I repeat the statement already made, that there is not a single passage in the Old Testament or New Testament where the Baptism with the Holy Spirit is spoken of or referred to where it is not connected with testimony or service.

The Baptism with the Holy Spirit is not primarily for the purpose of making us individually holy. Please note carefully my words and grasp exactly what I say. I do not say that it is not the work of the Holy Spirit to make us holy, for it is His work to make us holy, and it is only through His work that any one of us can become holy. I do say, however, that it is not *the primary purpose* of the *Baptism* with the Holy Spirit to make us holy. *The primary purpose of the Baptism with the Holy Spirit is to equip us and fit us for service.* This will become still clearer when we come to study the next part of our subject: the Results of the Baptism with the Holy Spirit.

Neither is it the primary purpose of the Baptism with the Holy Spirit to make us personally happy. Note again carefully what I say. I do not say that the Baptism with the Holy Spirit will not make us happy, if we receive it. I have never known anyone yet who was " baptized with the Holy Spirit " into whose heart a new and more wonderful joy did not come, but I am saying that *this is not the primary purpose of the Baptism with the Holy Spirit.* The primary purpose of the Baptism with the Holy Spirit is not to make us happy but to make us useful for God. I am glad that this is so, for while ecstacies are all right in their place, and while I know something about them in my own experience, yet in a world such as you and I live in, where there is this awful tide of men, women and children sweeping on unsaved to a hopeless eternity, I would rather go my entire life through without one single touch of ecstasy or rapture, and have power to do my part to stem this awful tide and save at least some, than to have indescribable raptures every day of my life and have no power to save the lost.

I wish to be very clear and very emphatic at this point, for here is where a multitude of people in our day are going astray. Men and women go off to " Bible Conferences," to " meetings for the deepening of the spiritual life," and to " tarrying meetings," and all that sort of thing, and they come back and tell you what a wonderful experience they have had, what raptures they have passed through, and how they have been " baptized with the Holy Spirit," and I have watched carefully a good many of these people; and many of them are of no more use to their pastors or their churches than they were before. And some of them are of far less use than they were before and are sometimes a positive nuisance. They have no more love for souls than they had before, make no more effort for the salvation of the lost than they did before, and win no more souls to Christ than they did before; and I am therefore sure that whatever experience they may have received they have not had the Baptism with the Holy Spirit along the lines so plainly laid down in God's own Word. So I repeat it again, THE BAPTISM WITH THE HOLY SPIRIT IS ALWAYS CONNECTED WITH, AND IS PRIMARILY FOR THE PURPOSE OF, EQUIPMENT FOR TESTIMONY AND SERVICE: IT IS TO MAKE US USEFUL FOR GOD IN THE SALVATION OF SOULS AND NOT MERELY TO MAKE US HAPPY.

II. THE RESULTS OF THE BAPTISM WITH THE HOLY SPIRIT

This leads us to the second question: What are the Results of the Baptism with the Holy Spirit? The results of the Baptism with the Holy Spirit as set forth in the Word of God are many-fold, but they can all be summed up in one word, and that word is POWER. This comes out in the passage to which I have already re-- ferred, Acts 1: 8: " YE SHALL RECEIVE POWER, when the Holy Ghost is come upon you: and ye shall be my wit- nesses both in Jerusalem, and in all Judea, and in Sa- maria, and unto the uttermost part of the earth."

Just as surely as anyone is baptized with the Holy Spirit he will have power, power for the work to which God has called him.   Just as surely as anyone here this af- ternoon meets the conditions of the Baptism with the Holy Spirit and is therefore " baptized with the Holy Spirit," there will come a new power into his life and service.

There needs, however, a word of caution to be said at this point, and not only to be said, but to be made clear and to be emphasized, and that word of caution is, this power will not manifest itself in the same way in every individual.   That thought is developed at considerable length in 1 Cor. 12, the classical passage on the whole subject of the Baptism with the Holy Spirit.   Let me read you verses 4 to 13: " Now there are *diversities of gifts,* but the same Spirit.   And there are *diversities of administrations,* but the same Lord.   And there are *di- versities of workings,* but the same God, Who worketh all things in all.   But *to each one* is given the manifesta- tion of the Spirit, to profit withal, for *to one* is given through the Spirit *the word of wisdom;* and *to another* the *word of knowledge,* according to the same Spirit; *to another, faith,* in the same Spirit; and *to another, gifts of healings,* in the one Spirit; *and to another, workings of miracles;* and *to another prophecy;* and *to another dis- cernings of spirits;* and *to another diverse kinds of tongues;* and *to another, interpretation of tongues;* but *all these* worketh the *one and the same Spirit,* dividing to each one *severally as He will.* For as the body is one, and hath many members, and all the members of the body, being many, are one body; so also is Christ. For *in one Spirit* were we all *baptized into one body,* whether Jews or Greeks, whether bond or free; and were *all* made to *drink of one Spirit."*

Now what strikes one, or what ought to strike one, most forcibly in this passage, is the word *"diversities"* so often repeated, and also the words *"to another"* so often repeated. And the thought is as clear as language can make it, and very much emphasized, that while there is "one Baptism with the Holy Spirit" there is a wide variety of manifestations of that one Baptism with that one and same Spirit; that *the Baptism with the Holy Spirit results in one gift in one person* according to the line of service to which he is called, *and quite another gift to another person,* according to the line of service to which he is called.

Now that is the point at which a multitude of people go astray. They hear of some person who was baptized with the Holy Spirit, and the Holy Spirit *for His own wise reasons* imparted to that person some special gift for the special service to which he was called, and they think that if they are baptized with the Holy Spirit they must have precisely the same gift that this other person had. But that is, as we see, entirely unscriptural; indeed, it is clearly anti-scriptural.

It was at this point that I was tempted to go astray when I first began the study of this subject, a great many years ago. I noticed that in the second chapter of the Acts of the Apostles, and in the tenth chapter of the Acts of the Apostles, and in the nineteenth chapter of the Acts of the Apostles, those who were baptized with the

Holy Spirit "spake with tongues," and I wondered if everyone who was baptized with the Holy Spirit would not speak with tongues. And as I did not see anyone speaking with tongues today, I wondered if this gift was not confined to the Apostolic Age. But one day my attention was called to First Corinthians the twelfth chapter, and I read the verses which I have just read to you, and discovered that while there was "one Baptism with the Holy Spirit," there was a vast variety of manifestations of that one baptism, and that it was distinctly said that to one was given "divers kinds of tongues," *but to others an entirely different gift;* and I also discovered that speaking with tongues was way down at the bottom of the list. And then my attention was fixed upon the closing verses of the chapter, verses 28 to 31, where I read: "And God *hath set some* in the church, *first* apostles, *secondly* prophets, *thirdly* teachers, *then* miracles, *then* gifts of healing, helps, governments, *divers kinds of tongues.*" Here again "tongues" was at the very bottom of the list. Then I went on and read: "Are all apostles? are all prophets? are all teachers? are all workers of miracles? Have all the gifts of healing? *do all speak with tongues?*" And therefore I saw that Paul clearly taught that there were among the believers in this wonderfully gifted church, of which he had plainly declared in the thirteenth verse *that every one of them was baptized with the Holy Spirit, some* at least *who did not speak with tongues.* So I saw that the teaching that speaking with tongues was the inevitable and invariable result of being baptized with the Holy Spirit, and that any one who had not spoken with tongues had not been baptized with the Holy Spirit, was utterly unscriptural and anti-scriptural.

But then I was tempted to fall into another error, of a somewhat similar character. I had read the testimony of John Wesley, and of Charles G. Finney, and D. L. Moody, and others, and I noted how all these men, when they were baptized with the Holy Spirit, obtained the gift of an evangelist, and I was tempted to say to myself, anyone who is baptized with the Holy Spirit will have the gift of an evangelist. Now that is just as unscriptural as to say that every one who is baptized with the Holy Spirit will speak with tongues. If God has called a man into the work of an evangelist, and he is baptized with the Holy Spirit, then doubtless he will have the gift of an evangelist, but if God has called him to some other work he will have some other power or gift, which will fit him for the work to which God has called him.

This mistake, that every one who is baptized with the Holy Spirit will have power as an evangelist, leads to three great evils. The first great evil to which it leads is the evil of disappointment, and sometimes even of despair. Many a man has heard an address upon the Baptism with the Holy Spirit which is not carefully guarded at this point, and he gets the impression that the inevitable and invariable result of the Baptism with the Holy Spirit is the gift of an evangelist, and then this man seeks for himself the Baptism with the Holy Spirit, and meets the conditions of that baptism, and consequently really is baptized with the Holy Spirit, but God has not called him to the work of an evangelist, and therefore, of course, God does not empower him with the gift of an evangelist, and the man is perplexed and bewildered and sometimes is in despair, wondering if he really has been baptized with the Holy Spirit.

I recall a very striking illustration of this. A Scotchman, a ship-plater, receiving large wages over in Scotland, heard an address on the Baptism with the Holy Spirit. He got the impression that the result of the Baptism with the Holy Spirit was in every instance power as an evangelist, and he sought for himself the Baptism with the Holy Spirit and obtained it. Then he heard that there were spiritually destitute fields in America, up in the Northwest, and he made up his mind to go there and preach the gospel; and at a great financial sacrifice he sold out everything and came out to Minnesota. But God had not at that time called him to be an evangelist, and he found no openings, and he was nearly in despair. He not only wondered whether he had been baptized with the Holy Spirit, he even got to doubting his salvation. While in this distressed state of mind, one Sunday morning, he dropped into the church in Minneapolis of which I was at that time pastor, and that very morning I spoke on the Baptism with the Holy Spirit, and made clear what I am trying to make clear to you today, that while " there is one Baptism " with the Holy Spirit, there is a wide diversity of manifestations of that one baptism; and that the gift of an evangelist is not by any means the invariable result of that baptism. He saw the truth and put himself in God's hands for God to choose the field of service and to qualify him for the service to which God had called him.

Very soon there came to him an opening to go down into some destitute parts of Wisconsin, doing Sunday School missionary work. He went, and there the great thing happened. When he had thus given up dictating to the Holy Spirit what gift should be bestowed upon him, and left it entirely with the Holy Spirit in His sovereign will to decide, and went out to do the work that God opened to him, the very gift that he had sought came upon him. He did receive the gift of an evangelist, and town after town was quite overturned by the power of the gospel as presented by him.

The second mischief that results from this error that the Baptism with the Holy Spirit will always result in power as an evangelist, is the error of presumption. Many a man has heard an address upon the Baptism with the Holy Spirit that is not carefully guarded at this point, and has gotten the impression that the one invariable result of the Baptism with the Holy Spirit is power as an evangelist, and so he says to himself, " All I need to become an evangelist is to receive the Baptism with the Holy Spirit. Now that is not true. It is very far from the truth. In order to be an evangelist the first thing a man needs is a call from God to that specific work. If God in His infinite wisdom has not called a man into that work, but into some other work, he certainly will not get power as an evangelist, even though he is baptized with the Holy Spirit. The second thing a man needs in order to be an evangelist is such a knowledge of the Word of God that he has something to preach that is worth listening to. If a man has a call of God to the work of an evangelist, and has obtained such a knowledge of the Word of God that he has something to preach that is worth listening to, and then is baptized with the Holy Spirit, he will have power as an evangelist, but otherwise he will not have power as an evangelist. One of the most unfortunate things in evangelistic work today is that so many men have rushed into the work whom God never called into it, who have no message that is worth while.

The third mischief that results from this error is the worst of all, and that is the mischief of indifference.

Many a person comes to a meeting like this and hears an address on the Baptism with the Holy Spirit and gets the impression that the one result of the Baptism with the Holy Spirit is the gift of an evangelist, and this person knows that God has not called him to the work of an evangelist. For instance, here is a woman, with a family of five or six or even more children. Now that woman knows, or at least it is to be hoped that she has sense enough to know, though some don't, that God has not called her to be an evangelist, that her work is at home with her children; and when she hears this address she says to herself, " My minister may need the Baptism with the Holy Spirit, the evangelist may need the Baptism with the Holy Spirit, the Y. M. C. A. Secretary may need the Baptism with the Holy Spirit, but I don't; for God has not called me to be an evangelist. My work is here at home with my own children." But if a mother gets the right conception of the Baptism with the Holy Spirit, the Bible conception, namely, that it is to fit believers in Jesus Christ not only for the work of an evangelist, but for any other function to which God may call us in His Church, and that there is no other function in the Church that God has more honoured than the function of sanctified motherhood, then this woman will say, " Evangelists may need the Baptism with the Holy Spirit, my pastor may need the Baptism with the Holy Spirit, but I must have it in order that I may have power to bring my own children up in the nurture and admonition of the Lord."

Before leaving this part of my subject, I wish to call your attention to the fact, and to emphasize the fact, that IT IS THE HOLY SPIRIT HIMSELF WHO DECIDES WHAT THE PARTICULAR GIFT OR MANIFESTATION SHALL BE IN

ANY GIVEN INSTANCE. This is very plain from 1 Cor. 12:11: "For all these worketh the one and the same Spirit, dividing to each one severally *even as He will.*" Here we are distinctly taught that it is not for us to choose some gift and look to the Holy Spirit to impart to us that self-chosen gift. It is not for us to choose for ourselves some field of service and look to the Holy Spirit to qualify us for the field of service which we have chosen. No, emphatically no! *It is for us to put ourselves entirely at the disposal of the Holy Spirit, for Him to choose the gift and for Him to qualify us with the gift which He has chosen; for Him to choose the field of service, and for Him to qualify us for the field of service which He Himself has chosen.* Oh, how many go astray at this point! They have chosen for themselves some particular gift, it may be speaking with tongues, it may be the gift of an evangelist, or some other gift, and then they meet the conditions of the Baptism with the Holy Spirit, and then, though they may not be definitely conscious of it, they try to dictate to the Holy Spirit what gift he shall impart to them. I have known people who have waited for weeks or months, or even years, for their self-chosen gift of speaking with tongues.

I recall a man whom I knew intimately in Chicago, a man who was very useful in his church and very gifted in prayer. While I was away, going around the world preaching the gospel, this man got under the influence of those people who over-emphasize "speaking with tongues." He gave up all his work and gave all his time, when he was not engaged in his business, to "*waiting for his Pentecost,*" by which he meant waiting until he should be enabled by the Spirit to speak with tongues.

After two long years of waiting, the last I knew of him he was still absolutely useless, " waiting for his Pentecost." No, No, No, the Holy Spirit is sovereign in the whole matter (1 Cor. 12:11), and it is not for you nor for me to dictate to Him what gift He shall impart to us when we are baptized with the Holy Spirit. It is for us to leave that entirely with Him, and just put ourselves unreservedly at His disposal, for Him to choose the field of service, and for Him to qualify us for the work to which He has called us, and to impart to us the gift that fits us for that work, whether it be speaking with tongues or something entirely different which, according to the repeated teaching of the Scriptures, is far more important than the least desirable of all gifts, that of " speaking with tongues."

But having given and emphasized this word of caution, let me repeat what I said some time ago, that *just as surely as anyone here today is baptized with the Holy Spirit, they will have a power in their service that they never had before; they will have power for the work to which God has called them.* I could stand here by the hour and repeat instances which have come under my own personal observation, of men and women and young people who have been baptized with the Holy Spirit, and who did " receive power." Let me give you three illustrations from life that I think will prove helpful.

The first is of a minister who was the first one, as far as I know definitely, that it was my privilege to lead into a like experience to my own. I had gone from Chicago to New Britain, Conn., more than a thousand miles, to deliver just one address. A thousand miles and back is a long ways to go to deliver one address, and yet I shall never cease to rejoice that I travelled that two thousand miles to deliver that address. It was at a State Convention of the Young People's Society of Christian Endeavour, held in an armory. Perhaps three thousand young people were present, and some older ones. I spoke upon the subject of Personal Work, and as I drew my address to a close I said, " In order to do efficient Personal Work one must be baptized with the Holy Spirit," and said a few words of explanation of what I meant by being " baptized with the Holy Spirit." When the convention closed a minister came to me on the platform and said, " I haven't this power that you have been talking about tonight, but I want it. Will you pray for me? " I replied, " Why not kneel down and pray right here now ? "

It is a good deal to ask of a Congregational minister in staid old New England, where the Congregationalists boast that they are the University denomination, and they are (for almost all the leading universities in New England were founded originally by the Congregationalists) —I say, it is a good deal to ask of a Congregational minister in staid old New England, to kneel down on a platform while three thousand young people are breaking up and leaving the armory in disorder, to seek a blessing from God like an old-fashioned Methodist inquirer at the mourners' bench; but this minister was in earnest, and he said, " I will." We placed two chairs together in a corner of the platform where we were not likely to be much observed, and knelt down to pray. I prayed and then he prayed that he might be baptized with the Holy Spirit. Then we arose and after a few words we had to separate, he to hurry to his train and I to hurry to mine.

Some time passed by and I was in Washington, D. C., at a Christian Workers' Convention. The night I reached

there I was standing in the rotunda of the hotel where
I was stopping, and an assistant pastor of the Fourth
Congregational Church in Hartford, Conn." saw me and
hurried to me and said, "Do you remember that minister that you prayed for at New Britain, Conn.?" I
said, "Yes, I do." He said, "Have you heard from him
since?" "No," I said. "Let me tell you about him,"
he said. "He has gone back to his church a transformed
man. He is pastor of a large country church in Connecticut, and since that night you prayed for him his
evening congregations fill his church, which," this man
added, "is a very unusual thing in a country church in
Connecticut. But that is not the best of it, there are
conversions at every service, and a very large proportion
of the conversions are the young men of the community."
Now is not that what we want? Not the sending off for
some evangelist to come at rare intervals and have some
great stirring of the community, but the power of God
upon the regular pastors of our churches, preaching in
the power of the Holy Spirit every Sunday night, and
conversions right along? Well, that is what we can have,
and the secret of it is the Baptism with the Holy Spirit.

Some years passed by and one hot summer afternoon
I was speaking at Mr. Moody's conference in Northfield,
Mass. I was speaking on Psalm 62: 11: "God hath
spoken once, twice have I heard this, that *power belong-
eth unto God.*" As I came down from the platform a
number of Methodist ministers from Alabama gathered
around me. They said, "Did we understand you to say
that if any minister did not have power and results in his
work it was his own fault?" "Well," I replied, "brethren, I am not sure that that is just what I said, but that
is about what I believe." "But," one of them urged,

"suppose your whole official board is against you. What can you do then?" Mr. G——, the Assistant Pastor of the church in Hartford, was there again, and he broke in, "Mr. Torrey, may I say something?" "Certainly," I replied.

He said, "Do you remember that Congregational minister that you prayed with at New Britain, Connecticut?" "Yes," I said, "I remember him well." He continued, "Did you know that he had changed his church?" "No, I did not." "Well," he said, "he did, last February." (This was August.) "He had a call from a church in the suburbs of Boston. All his spiritually minded friends advised him not to accept the call, for all the ruling members of the church were against aggressive evangelistic effort. But in spite of all the advice of his spiritually minded friends, he somehow felt led to accept the call, and he went there last February. There have already been fifty-nine conversions, and thirty-eight of them are business men of the community." Oh, brethren, is not that what we want? Well, that is the sort of thing we can have. The secret of it is in our being "baptized with the Holy Spirit."

Let me give you a second illustration. I had been at Montreal, Canada, attending an Inter-provincial Convention of the Young Men's Christian Association. In my last address I had spoken on the Baptism with the Holy Spirit. Sometime after I got back to Chicago, I received a letter from a young man, a member of one of the churches in Montreal. He wrote, saying:

"DEAR MR. TORREY:

"I was at your last meeting at the Y. M. C. A. convention in Montreal, and heard you speak on the baptism with the Holy Spirit. I went away to my home and sought that baptism for myself and obtained it. I am Chairman of the Lookout Committee of the Young People's Society of Christian Endeavour of our church. I got together the other members of our committee, and found that two of them had been at the same meeting, and had already obtained the baptism with the Holy Spirit. Then we prayed for the other members of the committee and they were baptized with the Holy Spirit; and now we are going out into the church among the young people, and the young people are coming to Christ right along."

Brethren, is not that what we want? Is not that what we want in our young people's societies? Not this everlasting getting up and quoting, parrot-like, some passage of Scripture; not this everlasting getting up at the monthly "Consecration Meeting" and professing to be wholly surrendered to God when you know you are not; but the young people of our churches baptized with the Holy Spirit, and going out among the other young people of the churches and communities, and leading them to Christ. Well, this is what we can have. The whole secret of it is having our young people "baptized with the Holy Spirit."

Now, just one more illustration, and to me in some respects the best of all. I was in Syracuse, N. Y., attending a Young Men's Christian Association State Convention. I was over speaking at the meeting of "the Women's Auxiliary." As I came down from the platform and passed out the door, a gentleman and his wife were waiting for me. They said, "Are you going over to the main meeting?" I said, "Yes." They said, "Are you going to walk?" I said, "Yes." "Can we walk with you?" "Yes," I said, "if you will walk fast." As we went down the stairs they began at once to tell me how they had never heard me before, but that they had read the report of an address that I had delivered at Boston, on the Baptism with the Holy Spirit, and they said, "We have been baptized with the Holy Spirit." Then the man did the talking. He was Superintendent of one of the prominent Sunday Schools of the city, and since he had been baptized with the Holy Spirit God had revolutionized the Sunday School. I heard from other sources that even the pastor of the church was transformed. When he had finished telling what the Baptism with the Holy Spirit had meant to him (and had also meant a transformed church), then his wife broke in and she said, "And, Mr. Torrey, the best part of it is that I have been able to get into the hearts of my own children, which I was never able to do before."

Oh, brethren, is not that what we want? Is not that what we must have? the power to get into the hearts of our own children, and to lead them to Christ? I think one of the saddest things in the Church of Jesus Christ today is to see the sons and daughters of the Christian fathers and mothers, fathers and mothers who have been pillars in the church, growing up not to follow in the footsteps of their fathers and mothers; growing up sometimes quite godless, not in the church on the Lord's Day, not in the Sunday School, but off joy-riding, or golfing, or on hiking parties, or playing tennis, or, God only knows what. Oh, the condition today of the children of earnest and godly and active Christian fathers and mothers, is appalling! What all of us fathers and mothers need, first of all, is power to get into the hearts of our own children. And we can have that power. Acts 1:8 tells us how: "Ye *shall receive power, when the Holy Ghost is come upon you.*"

Oh, men and women and young people who belong to

Christ! Are we having in our service for Christ the power that we might have and ought to have? We are living in a world where we are surrounded by perishing men, women and children on every hand. And there is a solemn responsibility upon every one of us, to do everything that is in our power, at any cost, to see that these men and women and children are saved. And there is a way in which any one of us can have power for that work. It is by being definitely baptized with the Holy Spirit. Shall we not decide today that, cost what it may, we will pay the price of that baptism and obtain it?

VI

THE BAPTISM WITH THE HOLY SPIRIT: WHO NEEDS IT AND WHO CAN HAVE IT.

WE saw yesterday that the Baptism with the Holy Spirit is a definite experience of which one may know whether he has received it or not.

We saw, in the second place, that the Baptism with the Holy Spirit is a work of the Holy Spirit distinct from and additional to the regenerating work of the Holy Spirit.

We saw, in the third place, that the Baptism with the Holy Spirit is always connected with and is primarily for the purpose of testimony and service.

We saw, in the fourth place, that the one great result of the Baptism with the Holy Spirit is POWER in the work to which God calls each one of us; that, while this power might manifest itself in a great variety of ways according to the different lines of service to which God has called us, there would always be power in the service of anyone who had been baptized with the Holy Spirit.

We come today to the very important question of the Necessity and Possibility of the Baptism with the Holy Spirit, or to put it in another way, Who Needs the Baptism with the Holy Spirit and Who Can Have It?

I. Who Needs the Baptism with the Holy Spirit?

We take up, first, the question of Who Needs the Baptism with the Holy Spirit? The Bible answers this question very plainly.

Turn first of all to Luke 24:49. We will begin back at the forty-fifth verse to get the connection: " Then opened He their minds, that they might understand the Scriptures ; and He said unto them, Thus it is written that Christ should suffer, and rise again from the dead the third day; and that repentance and remission of sins should be preached in His name unto all the nations, beginning from Jerusalem. Ye are witnesses of these things. And, behold, I send forth the promise of my Father upon you: but tarry ye in the city, until ye be clothed with power from on high."

Here our Lord gives a very definite, distinct and positive commandment to those to whom He was speaking, that they should not undertake the work to which He had called them until they had received the all-necessary preparation for that work of which He speaks here as " the promise of my Father upon you," and further on, as a being " clothed with power from on high," and by comparison of Scripture with Scripture we find that this " promise of the Father," this being " clothed with power from on high," is the Baptism with the Holy Spirit.

Now, to whom were these words spoken? To the eleven apostles. And who were those apostles? It is oftentimes said that they were uneducated men, and from that supposed fact an argument is adduced for an uneducated ministry. But no argument by any possibility could be more *mal-apropos* than that, for whatever the apostles were they were not uneducated men. They had taken more than a three-years' course in the best theological seminary that ever existed upon earth, and in which our Lord Jesus Christ Himself was the sole but all-sufficient

Teacher. They had been eye-witnesses of our Lord's wondrous life on earth, eye-witnesses of His miracles, eye-witnesses of His death, eye-witnesses of His resurrection from the dead, and they were about to be eye-witnesses of His ascension, as He was taken up into heaven bodily, right before their eyes, "and a cloud received Him out of their sight." And what were they to do? Simply to go and tell a perishing world what their own eyes had seen and what their own ears had heard from the lips of the Son of God Himself. Were they not already fully prepared to go? With our modern ideas of preparation for the ministry we should say they were the most fully and perfectly prepared and equipped men who ever undertook the ministry of the Gospel. But our Lord Jesus here says: You are not adequately prepared at all; there is another preparation so all-necessary that you must not stir one step until you have obtained it. That preparation is the receiving of "the promise of the Father," the being "endued with power from on high," the Baptism with the Holy Spirit. "And till you receive it, do not undertake that ministry." The word translated "tarry," means literally "sit down": "Sit down, until ye be clothed with power from on high." This is exceedingly solemn. If our Lord would not permit the men whom He Himself had chosen and ordained for this work to undertake that work until they had received a definite enduement of power from on high for that service, namely, the Baptism with the Holy Spirit, what is it for ordinary mortals like you or me to undertake that service until we are thus baptized by the Holy Spirit and know it? It is the most daring presumption.

One of the gravest mistakes that the Church of Jesus Christ is making today is in the way in which we set men apart for the ministry of the Gospel. We take a man who is "hopefully pious," send him for four years to a college, then three or four years to a theological seminary, and then, if he has succeeded in coming out of these in-situation with a fair *modicum* of faith left, we say, "You are now fitted to undertake the ministry," and we lay our hands upon him and set him apart for this solemn work. But is he prepared? He certainly is not, if that is all he has. It would be a great thing if to every candidate for the ministry, before ordaining him, we should put to him the question: "Are you sure you have been clothed with power from on high? Are you sure you have been baptized with the Holy Spirit?" And if he were not sure, we should say to him: "Sit down, until you are clothed with power from on high."

But this is not all; nor, solemn as it is, is it the most solemn part. Turn in your Bibles to Acts 10: 38: "God anointed Jesus of Nazareth with the Holy Ghost and with power; who went about doing good, and healing all that were oppressed of the devil; for God was with Him." To what definite experience does this refer in the life of our Lord as recorded in the Gospels? Turn to the Gospel of Luke, the third chapter, twenty-first and twenty-second verses, and you will get your answer: "Now it came to pass, when all the people were baptized, that Jesus also having been baptized, and praying, the heaven was opened and the Holy Spirit descended in a bodily form, as a dove upon him, and a voice came out of heaven, Thou art my beloved Son; in Thee I am well pleased." Now turn to the next chapter, the fourth, and the first verse,—nothing in-tervening but the genealogy of His mother: "And Jesus, *full of the Holy Spirit,* returned from the Jordan." Now turn to the fourteenth and following verses, the story of

His temptation being all that intervenes, and read again:
" And Jesus returned *in the power of the Spirit* into Gali-
lee, and fame went out concerning Him through all the
region round about, and He taught in their synagogues,
being glorified of all. And He came to Nazareth, where
He had been brought up: and He entered, as His custom
was, into the synagogue on the Sabbath day, and stood
up to read. And there was delivered unto Him the book
of the prophet Isaiah. And He opened the book and
found the place where it was written: *The Spirit of the
Lord is upon me,* because He *anointed* me to preach good
tidings to the poor: He hath sent me to proclaim release
to the captives, and recovery of sight to the blind, to set
at liberty them that are bruised, to proclaim the acceptable
year of the Lord. And He closed the book, and gave it
back to the attendant, and sat down: and the eyes of all in
the synagogue were fastened on Him."

From these verses we learn that it was at the Jordan
that our Lord was endued with power from on high, that
He was baptized with the Holy Spirit, and *after that, and
not till after that,* He began His public ministry.

And who was our Lord? He was " The only begotten
Son of God." He was God manifest in the flesh, He was
" very God of very God." He had been supernaturally
conceived by the power of the Holy Spirit, but He was at
the same time man, and as a man setting an example to
you and me to follow in His steps, He never undertook
the public ministry, for which He came into this world,
until He had been definitely " endued with power from on
high." Now listen: If our Lord Jesus, though He had
been supernaturally conceived by the power of the Holy
Spirit, though He was the Word of God made flesh,
though He " was God," (Jno. 1:1), though in Him

"dwelt all the fulness of the Godhead bodily" (Clos. 2:9), did not permit Himself to undertake His public ministry until He was definitely "endued with power from on high," what is it for ordinary mortals, such as you and I are, to undertake service for Him until we also are thus endued and know it? To ME IT APPEARS LIKE THE MOST DARING PRESUMPTION; yes, something even beyond that. In view of what the Lord required of His apostles, and still more in view of what He required of Himself, I dare not undertake service for Him until I, too, have been baptized with the Holy Spirit and know it.

But even that is not all. If you will turn to Acts 8: 12-17, you will find that the apostles, when they came to a new church that had just been gathered, the very first thing they always saw to was that all the members of this new church "might receive the Holy Spirit." And if you will turn to Acts 19: 1-6, you will find that the Apostle Paul, when he came to a community where there was a young church, and where he discovered something about it that was not satisfactory, the first thing that he inquired into was whether they had definitely "received the Holy Spirit."

IN THE LIGHT OF ALL THESE FACTS, WE ARE ABUN- DANTLY WARRANTED IN SAYING THAT EVERY CHILD OF GOD IS UNDER THE MOST SOLEMN OBLIGATION TO SEE TO IT THAT HE DEFINITELY RECEIVES THE HOLY SPIRIT, NOT MERELY AS A REGENERATING POWER AND AS AN INDWELL- ING PRESENCE, BUT AS A DEFINITE ENDUEMENT WITH POWER, BEFORE HE UNDERTAKES SERVICE OF ANY KIND FOR GOD.

Let me say further that, no matter how definitely one may have been baptized with the Holy Spirit, he needs a new filling with the Holy Spirit for each new emergency of Christian service. We are told of the Apostle Peter in Acts 2:4 that he was definitely "filled with the Holy Spirit" on the day of Pentecost. But in Acts 4:8 we are also told that "Peter" was again "filled with the Holy Spirit." The tense of the verb used in the original (that is, in the Greek), shows conclusively that the filling spoken of here was a new filling that took place right then and there. But we are again told in Acts 4:31 that "When they had prayed, the place was shaken wherein they were gathered together: and *they were all filled with the Holy Spirit,* and they spake the Word of God with boldness." Here again the tense of the verb used in the original, that is, in the Greek, shows conclusively that it was a filling that took place right then and there. And we are definitely told that Peter was one of the "all" who were then and there filled with the Holy Spirit.

So here are three separate occasions on which Peter was "filled with the Holy Spirit." So then it is as clear as day that one needs repeated fillings with the Holy Spirit, no matter how definitely and wonderfully he may have been baptized with the Holy Spirit in the past. *We need to be filled again and again,* filled anew for each new emergency of Christian service. I am often asked if I have received "The Second Blessing." I certainly have, —and the third and the fourth and the fifth and the three hundredth and the three hundred and fortieth, and I am looking for the three hundred and forty-first today. One of the commonest mistakes today, and one of the gravest, is that many people are trying to work today in the power of some baptism with the Spirit that they received a year ago, or two years ago, or five years ago, or ten years ago, as the case may be. Don't make that mistake. However definitely you may have been "baptized with the Holy

Spirit " in the past you need, you must have, a new in-filling for each new emergency of Christian service. And you must seek it in God's appointed way—by prayer (Luke 11 : 13), definite prayer for a definite blessing.

A good many years ago, when I was the president of the International Convention of Christian Workers, we held a meeting in the city of Detroit. I think it was our third annual gathering. I had a friend who had been led out into an experience of the Holy Spirit's infilling that he had never had before through a well-known teacher in this country. He asked that I put this teacher on the program of the Detroit Convention. This I did. But to my dismay, when I reached Detroit I found that he was circulating a paper of his in which he took the ground that when one was once baptized with the Holy Spirit that ended it; there was nothing more to seek. When he himself came to speak, his utterances were utterly without power. He himself most manifestly needed a new filling with the Holy Spirit.

During the World's Fair in Chicago, in 1893, Mr. Moody brought together, in Chicago, some of the most renowned and most able Bible teachers and Gospel preach-ers from all parts of the world. He said: " For years I have been going to the world; now the world is coming to me, and I am going to see that they get the Gospel through the best preachers in their different languages that I can secure." He brought famous men from Eng-land, Scotland, Ireland, France, Germany, Austria, Rus-sia and other lands. Among others, he brought a man who had been wonderfully used in his own country. He took this man first to Northfield, and then brought him on to Chicago. When he was giving his first lecture in the lecture-room of the Bible Institute in Chicago, Mr.

Moody said to me: "I want you to hear this man and give me your opinion of him." So when the crowd had gathered we slipped into a back seat where we would not be seen. After listening for a while, Mr. Moody slipped out and beckoned me to follow. We went up to his office and sat down. Mr. Moody turned to me and said: "What do you think of him?" I replied: "I have nothing I wish to say." "Well," he said, "I have something I wish to say: I would give every penny it cost me to bring him to this country if he were back home again. He has lost his unction!"

Oh, it is an awful thing to lose one's unction! Mr. Moody used to say that he would rather die than to lose the power of the Holy Spirit in his work. But we certainly shall lose our unction unless we seek a new filling with the Spirit for each new emergency of Christian service.

I am often asked: "Would you call these new fillings with the Holy Spirit 'fresh baptisms with the Holy Spirit?'" No, I would not. I would not for two reasons: First of all, because there is something initiatory in the very thought conveyed by the word "baptism:" and second, because these new fillings are never called "baptisms" in the Bible, and it is always wise to hold fast to Bible terminology. In the Bible the expression "baptized with the Holy Spirit" is always limited to the first experience of the individual. But I would much rather that people would speak of "fresh baptisms with the Holy Spirit" because they recognized that one cannot go in the power of a baptism with the Holy Spirit received some time before, but needs a new filling for each new emergency of Christian service, than that they be such sticklers for exact terminology that they lose sight of the imperative need of new fillings with the Spirit for each new emergency of Christian service. In other words, I would rather have the right thing by the wrong name than the wrong thing by the right name.

II. Who Can Have the Baptism with the Holy Spirit?

We come now to the very practical and immeasurably important question: Who can have the Baptism with the Holy Spirit? Some years ago I was speaking at a convention in the state of Kansas, and a woman who was one of the leaders in church work in that state and who was also in a high position in the educational work of the state, sent me a little note in which she said: " You have spoken about the necessity of being baptized with the Holy Spirit. Will you kindly tell me who can be thus baptized? The church to which I belong teaches that the Baptism with the Holy Spirit was confined to the days of the apostles." Well, who can be baptized with the Holy Spirit? We are not left to speculate about that. God Himself answers the question in the plainest possible words. Turn in your Bibles to Acts 2: 39, and you will get God's own answer to this all important question: " For *the promise is unto you,* and *to your children,* and *to all that are afar off, even as many as the Lord our God shall call."*

What is the " promise " to which Peter refers in this verse? Doubtless many of you know that there are two differing interpretations of this verse. One interpretation is that " the promise " of this verse is the promise of salvation and that the verse therefore sets forth the Covenant privilege of believers to have their children saved. Now, no one believes in the Covenant privilege of believers to have their children saved more firmly than I do, but is that the meaning of this verse?

The other interpretation is that "the promise" of this verse is the promise of the "gift of," (or, to put it in other words, "the baptism with") the Holy Spirit." Which of these two interpretations is correct?

There are two laws of interpretation universally accepted by all rational, or really intelligent, interpreters of the Word. The first law is called "the law of the *usus loquendi.*" The other law is "the law of context."

The law of the *usus loquendi* (or, to use plain English, which is far better than Latin, "the law of usage"), is that when you find a word or phrase in the Bible and you wish to know exactly what it means, the thing to do is not to run for a dictionary to get the definition of the word or phrase, for the dictionary was not written by Bible scholars. The thing to do is to take your concordance and look up every place in the Bible where that word or phrase is used and interpret its meaning by its usage. The exact meaning of words is seldom determined by etymology; it is determined by usage.

Now, what is the usage of this phrase, "the promise," in the Bible, especially what is the usage in this particular book in the Bible in which this verse is found? Turn back to Acts 1:4 and 5: "He charged them not to depart from Jerusalem, but to wait for *the promise of the Father,* which, said He, ye heard from me: for John indeed baptized with water: but *ye shall be baptized with the Holy Spirit* not many days hence." What "the promise" is here we are not left to guess. We are told that "the promise" is "the promise" of being "baptized with the Holy Spirit." Now turn to Acts 2:33: "Being therefore by the right hand of God exalted and having received of the Father *the promise of the Holy Spirit,* He hath poured forth this which ye see and hear." Here again we are told that " the promise of the Father " is " the promise of the Holy Spirit " which had just been poured forth on that very day when every one of the apostolic company had been baptized with the Holy Spirit. In other words the meaning of the expression is precisely the same here as it was in the first chapter. Now, six verses further down we come to the verse we are now studying. Can anyone tell me any reasonable rule of interpretation by which this peculiar expression can mean one thing in Acts 1: 4 and 5, precisely the same thing in the next place where it occurs, that is, Acts 2: 33, and something entirely different in the next place where it occurs, only six verses further down? *Beyond any possible intelligent question, the phrase " the promise of the Father," in Acts 2: 39, refers to the Baptism with the Holy Spirit.* The law of the *usus loquendi,* even if it stood alone, would settle the question, but it does not stand alone.

Let us now apply the law of context. The law of context is this: That when you find a passage of Scripture of which there are two or more possible interpretations and you wish to know which one of the several different interpretations is the correct interpretation, you should look at the passage in its context, that is, in the light of what goes before it and in the light of what comes after it. Many a passage in the Bible, if it stood alone, might mean one, two, three, four or even more things. But standing where it does, it can mean but one of the two or more things.

Now let us apply the law of context here. Let us read what goes immediately before—vs. 38: " Peter said unto them, Repent ye and be baptized, every one of you, in the name of Jesus Christ, unto the remission of your sins: and *ye shall receive the gift of the Holy Spirit. For to you is the promise,* and to your children, and to all that are afar off, even as many as the Lord our God shall call unto Him." Here Peter in the preceding verse declares exactly what the promise is to which he refers. He says: " Ye shall receive *the gift of the Holy Spirit. For to you is the promise,* and to your children, and to all that are afar off, even as many as the Lord our God shall call unto Him." The promise, then, is unmistakably the promise of the " gift of " (or, to use the synonymous phrase, " the baptism with ") " the Holy Spirit." *The two laws therefore agree and they both determine, beyond the possibility of intelligent question, that the promise of Acts 2: 39 is the promise of the gift of, or baptism with, the Holy Spirit.* Let us then read the verse in the light of this settled fact: " For to you is the promise,"—that is, to the people whom he was addressing, who were for the most part Jews. Thus far there is nothing in it for you or me, for we were not there, and we are not Jews. But Peter did not stop there: " And to your children," that is, to the next generation of Jews, or, if you will, to all coming generations of Jews, and that does not take many of us in. But, thank God, Peter did not stop there, but added: " And *to all that are afar off."* That does take us in, for we are the Gentiles who were " once afar off, but are now made nigh by the blood of Christ " (Eph. 2: 13). But lest there be any doubt about it, Peter does not stop even there, but adds: " *Even as many as the Lord our God shall call unto him"* (R. V.) ; that is the call not merely to service, but the call to salvation. We are thus here told in plain words, the meaning of which is unmistakable, that the Baptism with the Holy Spirit is for every child of God, in every age of the Church's history. THE BAPTISM WITH THE HOLY SPIRIT IS THE BIRTH-RIGHT OF EVERY BELIEVER IN JESUS CHRIST. It is true that not every believer has claimed his brithright, but it is his, promised by God and provided by God, through a crucified, risen and ascended Saviour, and if you have not claimed your birthright, it is your own fault, and you may claim it today.

Some years ago we had for a month a Ministerial Institute in the Bible Institute of Chicago. Ministers were gathered there from very many different states of our Union, and for a month we studied the Word of God together. At the closing session of the Institute, I spoke on the " Baptism with the Holy Spirit," and emphasized the necessity of it if we were to do acceptable service for God. At the close of the meeting a minister from the state of Texas came to me and said: " The church to which I belong teaches that the Baptism with the Holy Spirit was only for the apostles. What do you think?" I replied: " I don't care what the church to which you belong teaches, nor what the church to which I belong teaches; the only question with me is, What does the Word of God teach?" He said: " That is right." " Well," I said, " take it and look at it," and I handed him my Bible open at Acts 2: 39, and asked him to read. And he read: " For the promise is unto you, and to your children, and to all that are afar off, even as many as the Lord our God shall call." I said: " Has He called you? Are you a saved man?" He replied: " I am." " Then is the promise for you?" He replied: " It must be." He claimed it. He went back to his pastorate in Texas, a transformed man. For years I received letters from him telling me how God was blessing him in his work.

It is for you, too, if you will claim it and meet the conditions of receiving it.

Let me illustrate this point again: I was at one of the early Y. M. C. A. conventions of the Students of Southern Colleges and Universities, held at Knoxville, Tennessee, on the university grounds. The meeting was presided over by Dr. ——, a very prominent and highly honored and much loved rector of the Protestant Episcopal Church. I spoke on the closing Sunday morning upon the Baptism with the Holy Spirit. This Episcopal rector and I roomed in the same building, and on that hot July afternoon we drew our chairs up in front of the building for a talk together. He turned to me and said: " I was greatly interested in what you had to say this morning, and if your interpretation of Acts 2: 39 is correct you have gained your case. But I question your interpretation of Acts 2: 39. Let us talk it over." And we did. Some years later I was at the Y. M. C. A. Student Convention at Northfield, Massachusetts, and this Episcopal rector was also present. One Sunday afternoon I entered Stone Hall, where the meetings were held in those days, by the back door, just as this Episcopal rector was entering through the front door, and we met. As he saw me approaching, he hurried toward me with extended hand, and said: " You were right about Acts 2: 39, at Knoxville; but I think I can tell you something better than that, I think I have now the right to say that I have been baptized with the Holy Spirit." I thank God that I was right. Not because it was at all important that I should be right, but because the doctrine is such a glorious one. Oh, to be able to go round this globe and face audiences of thousands—Americans, English, Scotch, Irish, Germans, Scandinavians, Russians, French, Swiss,

Hindus, Japanese, Chinese, and others, as I have done, and to be able to tell them all, with the absolute certainty that you have God's own immutable word supporting you when you tell them, that the Baptism with the Holy Spirit is for every one of them. What marvellous scenes I have seen, as believers in many lands have seen this truth and claimed for themselves the wondrous blessing of the Baptism with the Holy Spirit; yes, and what marvellous results have followed in many lands.

But this glorious truth has its solemn side. If each one of us may be—and beyond a question we may—baptized with the Holy Spirit, then there rests upon us the most solemn obligation to be thus baptized. It is not merely a matter of privilege; it is a matter of most solemn duty. If you and I pay the price of this blessing it will be ours and souls will be won to Christ who will not be thus won if we do not pay the price and therefore do not obtain the blessing; and if we do not pay the price and therefore do not obtain the blessing, we shall be responsible before God for everyone that might have been saved who was not saved because we did not pay the price and therefore did not obtain the blessing.

Beloved brethren, I oftentimes tremble for myself and for others who are in the ministry. And by the ministry I do not mean merely the ministry as ordinarily defined, as including only ordained ministers. I use it in the broader sense applying to all believers, for we are all called to minister the Gospel in some way. It may not be by preaching; it may be in quiet, humble, personal work. I say I tremble for myself and for my brethren in the ministry. Why? Because we are preaching error? Oh, no, I do not mean that now. It is true there are many in these days who claim to be preaching the truth who are preaching in reality the most pernicious and destructive error, and I do tremble for them: I would rather take my chance before the bar of God as a bootlegger than to take my chance there as one who is called to preach the Gospel, but who, instead, was preaching error —damnable and destructive error. But that is not what I refer to now.

Do I mean that I tremble for those who are not preaching error, but are not preaching the truth? For you all know it is quite possible for a man never to preach a word of error and yet not preach the saving truth. There are many, many ministers nowadays from whose lips a heterodox word has never escaped, and yet they are not preaching the truth. They are preaching on all kinds of extraneous and unimportant questions. Take any daily paper that announces the subjects to be preached upon in any of our great cities, and your heart will certainly be heavy with sadness if you are at all thoughtful. In one of our American cities some time ago these three subjects were announced in the same newspaper by different prominent preachers in that city: " The Wit of an Irishman," " The Football Match," " My Mother-in-Law." Horrible! Think of it! Standing in the sacred desk, the place of such marvellous opportunity and possibility of power for God, and preaching on subjects like that! Yes, I do tremble for these faithless and foolish shepherds.

But that is not what I mean now. What I mean is this: I tremble for those who are preaching the Gospel— preaching the Gospel in its simplicity, in its purity and in its fullness, but preaching it " with enticing words of man's wisdom," and not " in demonstration of the Spirit and of power " (1 Cor. 2:4). Oh, a man may preach the most sound and most able orthodoxy and preach his audience right into hell! *The deadest thing on earth is dead orthodoxy!* IT IS NOT ENOUGH THAT WE PREACH THE GOSPEL, NOT ENOUGH THAT WE PREACH IT IN ITS SIMPLICITY, ITS PURITY, ITS FULLNESS, BUT WE MUST PREACH IT IN THE POWER OF THE HOLY SPIRIT. And we can do this only insofar as we are definitely baptized with the Holy Spirit and insofar as we are definitely filled again and again with His glorious power for each new emergency of Christian service. I repeat again, if we pay the price of this blessing and are therefore baptized with the Holy Spirit and filled again and again with His Divine power as we preach, there will be souls won to Christ through our ministry, whether it be through the ministry of public preaching or the ministry of personal work, who will not be thus won if we do not pay the price and therefore do not obtain the blessing, and therefore if we do not pay the price of this blessing and consequently do not obtain it, we shall be responsible before God for every one who might have been saved but who was not saved because we did not pay the price and therefore did not obtain the blessing. We must be, *we must be,* WE MUST BE *baptized with the Holy Spirit.*

Tomorrow we shall take up the price of obtaining this blessing. Or, to put it in other words, we shall take up the question of just what each one of us must do to make it sure that we shall be baptized with the Holy Spirit; and, if we have already been thus baptized with the Holy Spirit, how we may be filled again and again with His glorious presence and power.

VII

THE BAPTISM WITH THE HOLY SPIRIT: HOW TO OBTAIN IT

WE have seen that the Baptism with the Holy Spirit is a definite experience of which one may know whether he has received it or not; that it is a work of the Holy Spirit distinct from and in addition to His regenerating work; that is is always connected with and is primarily for the purpose of testimony and service and that the one great result of that baptism is power in the work to which God calls us. We have also seen that the Baptism with the Holy Spirit is absolutely necessary for acceptable service and effective work for God. And we also saw yesterday that it is the privilege of every believer in every age of the Church's history to have the Baptism with the Holy Spirit and that a most solemn responsibility rests upon every one of us to obtain it at any cost. We have seen that if we pay the price of this blessing and therefore obtain it there will be souls won to Christ through our work who, if we do not pay the price of this blessing and therefore do not obtain it, will not be thus won; and that therefore if we do not pay the price of this blessing and therefore do not obtain it, we shall be responsible before God for every one who might have been won but was not won because we did not pay the price and therefore did not obtain the blessing.

This brings us face to face with the all-important question, "What must we do in order that we may obtain the Baptism with the Holy Spirit?" It is a question of tremendous importance; but it is a question that is very plainly answered in the Word of God. There is a very plain path laid down in God's Word, consisting of a few simple steps that anyone can take, and IT IS ABSOLUTELY CERTAIN THAT ANY ONE WHO TAKES THESE STEPS WILL BE "BAPTIZED WITH THE HOLY SPIRIT."

That is a very positive statement and I would not dare be thus positive if the Word of God were not equally positive, but when the Word of God definitely and distinctly says that if you do certain things there will be a certain result, what right have we to tone down the positiveness of God's Word and say that if we do certain things there will "probably" be a certain result?

If any one should come to me and ask me, "Can you tell me what to do right now and here, and guarantee that if I do it I will be saved at once?" Without the slightest hesitation I would reply, "I can." I can tell any one what to do right now and guarantee that if they do it, they will be saved instantly. If I could not tell you that, I would not be fit to be preaching the Gospel. And just so, if any one should come to me and say, "Dr. Torrey, can you tell me what to do right here and now and guarantee that if I will do it, I will be baptized with the Holy Ghost?", without the slightest hesitation I would reply, "I can." I can, because the Bible tells us in the plainest possible terms that very thing. It tells us that if we do certain things which are clearly defined in the Bible, we "*shall receive the gift of the Holy Spirit.*" What right, then, have we to qualify God's statement and say that if we do certain things we shall probably receive the gift of (or, the baptism with) the Holy Spirit?

It is oftentimes said that Dr. Torrey is a very dogmatic preacher. I trust that the charge is true. I aim to be a dogmatic preacher. I aim to be just as dogmatic as this Book. I do not think that I have attained to that as yet, but that is my aim, and if this Book says in the most positive and dogmatic terms that if you do certain things you shall be baptized with the Holy Spirit, I do not hesitate to affirm without the slightest fear that my affirmation will prove untrue, that any one here who does these certain things, who takes these certain steps, will be immediately " baptized with the Holy Spirit."

THERE IS A PLAIN PATH, CONSISTING OF SEVEN VERY SIMPLE STEPS, WHICH ANY ONE HERE CAN TAKE TODAY, AND IT IS ABSOLUTELY SURE THAT ANY ONE WHO TAKES THOSE SEVEN STEPS WILL ENTER INTO THE BLESSING. You will find all seven steps in Acts 2: 38. I shall later refer to other passages that throw more light upon this passage and make some of the steps clearer, but they are all in this passage.

Let me read the passage: " Then Peter said unto them, Repent ye, and be baptized every one of you, in the name of Jesus Christ unto the remission of your sins; and *ye shall receive the gift of the Holy Ghost.*"

Now, Peter's statement here is just as positive as mine. He says if we do certain things, the result will be that we " shall receive the gift of the Holy Ghost." What right, then, have we to say that if we do these things, perhaps we may receive the gift of the Holy Ghost? There is no perhaps about it. We certainly shall.

The First Step. The first two steps are found in the word " Repent." What does repentance mean? Doubtless many of you have been told time after time that *Repentance* is a Change of Mind. When you were told that, you were told the exact truth. But a change of mind about what? A change of mind about three things: a change of mind about God, a change of mind about Jesus Christ, a change of mind about sin. What the change of mind is about in any given instance must be determined by the context. *As determined by the context in this case, the change of mind is primarily about Jesus Christ.* In the thirty-sixth verse we read: "Let all the house of Israel therefore know assuredly, that God hath made Him both Lord and Christ, this Jesus whom ye crucified," and we read in verse thirty-seven: "Now when they heard this, they were pricked in their heart, and said unto Peter and the rest of the apostles, 'Brethren, what shall we do?'", and then we read verse thirty-eight: "And Peter said unto them, 'Repent ye'"—that is, change your mind about Jesus Christ, change from that attitude of mind that rejected Christ and crucified Christ to that attitude of mine that accepts Jesus Christ as Saviour and Lord. *This, then, is the first step toward receiving the Baptism with the Holy Spirit—accept Jesus Christ as Saviour and Lord.*

First of all, *Accept Jesus as Saviour.* Have you thus accepted Him? If I should go down from this platform and go to you as you sit there in the seats, one after another, and put to you the question, "Have you received Jesus Christ as your Saviour?" I think that most of you would reply, "Yes, I have." But suppose I should put to you a second question, "Upon what are you resting as the ground of your acceptance before God?"—I am sure some of you would answer me something like this, "Why, I go to church, I read my Bible, I have been baptized, I have joined the church (or, been confirmed, as the case may be), I go regularly to church, I partake of the communion, I give a tenth of my income to the church or the poor, and I am trying to live just as near right as I know how." Well, if that is what you are resting upon as the ground of your salvation, you are not saved. All those things are your works; good things in their place, but every one of them your own works, and God tells us plainly in His Word, in Romans 3:20, "*By the works of the law* shall no flesh be justified in His sight"; therefore if these are the things you are trusting in as the ground of your acceptance before God, you are not justified, you are not saved.

But if I should go to some of you and put to you the question, "Are you saved?" you would reply at once, "Yes, I am," and if then I should put to you the second question, "On what are you resting as the ground of your salvation?", you would reply something like this: "I am not resting upon anything I have done or anything I am ever going to do, *I am resting entirely upon what Jesus Christ did when He bore my sins in His own body on the cross. If that is true,* then you are saved, and *you have taken the first step toward receiving the Baptism with the Holy Spirit.* THE FIRST STEP, THEN, TOWARD RECEIVING THE BAPTISM WITH THE HOLY SPIRIT IS THAT WE REST ENTIRELY UPON THE FINISHED WORK OF JESUS CHRIST ON THE CROSS OF CALVARY, UPON HIS ATONING DEATH FOR US, AS THE SOLE GROUND OF OUR ACCEPTANCE BEFORE GOD.

This thought comes out again and again in the Bible. We find it, for example, very plainly stated in Galatians 3:2. In this passage, Paul says: "This only would I learn from you, Received ye the Spirit by the works of the law, or by the hearing of faith?" What does Paul mean by this? On one occasion Paul was passing through

Galatia and was detained there by some physical infirmity. We are not told what it was; presumably it was some trouble with his eyes. But that does not matter for our present purpose. At all events, he was not so ill that he could not preach and he did preach to these Galatians. He preached to them that Christ had redeemed us from the curse of the law by becoming a curse in our place (Gal. 3:13), and that by simple faith in Him Who died in their place, all their sins were forgiven and they were justified from all things (2 Cor. 5:21; Acts 13:38, 39). The Galatians believed this proclamation of the Gospel and put their trust in the atoning death of Jesus Christ on the cross as their ground of acceptance before God, and God immediately set His seal to their faith by giving them as a conscious, experimental possession, the Holy Spirit. But after Paul had gone away, certain men came down from Jerusalem who mixed up the Jewish law with the simple Gospel of Christ and told these people, these believers in Galatia, that merely believing in Jesus Christ was not enough, that in addition to that, if they were to be saved, they must be circumcised according to the law of Moses. (Just as the Seventh Day Adventist people come along nowadays and tell young Christians that it is not enough to believe in the Lord Jesus Christ, that in addition to that, they must keep the seventh day Sabbath according to the law of Moses. It is the same old controversy, only breaking out at a new point.)

These young believers in Galatia were all upset. They did not know whether they were saved (or, justified) or not. This reaches the ears of the Apostle Paul and he is very indignant. Nothing makes true Christian workers more indignant, nor more righteously indignant, than to have false teachers come along and try to upset young converts and get them confused. So he wrote this epistle to the Galatians to show the Galatian believers the truth and expose the error of these Judaizers. I am glad that these Judaizers came down, for, while they upset these Galatian believers for a while, the ultimate outcome was good, for it gave rise to this wonderful epistle to the Galatians, which is the greatest exposition of the doctrine of justification by faith that is to be found in the Bible, even greater on this one point than the epistle to the Romans.

First of all, Paul called the attention of the young believers in Galatia to the fact that Abraham himself was justified before he was circumcised, that "Abraham (simply) believed God" and his simply believing God was "counted unto him for righteousness" (Gal. 3:6). He showed them that after Abraham was thus *justified by simple faith,* he was circumcised, *not in order to be justified,* but as "*a seal of the faith that he had while he was still in uncircumcision*" (Romans 4:11, R. V.).

Then Paul exposes the error of these Judaizers in a second way. He appeals directly to the experience of the believers in Galatia. He says to them, in effect, "You received the Holy Spirit, did you not, as a definite experience?" "Yes, Paul, we did." "Well, then," he says in substance, "let me ask you a question? How did you receive the Holy Spirit—'by works of the law' (that is, by keeping the Mosaic law) or by 'the hearing of faith' (that is, by simply believing God's testimony about Jesus Christ, that He had borne their sins in His own body on the cross and by simply trusting God to forgive their sins because Jesus Christ had died in their place)?" And they replied, "Why, of course, Paul, we received the Holy Spirit by the 'hearing of faith.'" And that is the way every one of us must receive Him. This, then, is the very first step, the most fundamental step of all in receiving the Baptism with the Holy Spirit, to rest absolutely on the finished work of Jesus Christ on the cross as the sole ground of our acceptance before God. When we do thus receive Jesus Christ, the Baptism with the Holy Spirit becomes our birthright.

Some years ago an engineer on the Rock Island Railroad was converted in the Moody church in Chicago. Not long after this, one of the well-instructed members of the church was crossing the Rock Island Railroad tracks in the south part of Chicago and this engineer came down the track on a switch engine. He saw this other man about to cross the track and slowed down the engine and said, " John, don't you want to take a ride? " He replied, " Yes," and climbed up into the cab with the engineer. They had not gone very far when Mr. Morrison began to draw the young convert out. After the young convert had talked some time, Mr. Morrison said quietly to him, " You have a different religion from mine." " What, John," he said, "a different religion from yours? I thought we had the same religion." " No," Mr. Morrison replied, "you have a different religion from mine. You have a religion of two letters. I have a religion of four letters." " What do you mean, John? " the man asked. John replied, " Your religion is D-O, DO ; you are all the time talking about what you do. My religion is D-O-N-E, DONE, I am trusting to what Jesus Christ has done, when He bore my sins in His own body on the cross." That, let me repeat, is the first step toward receiving the Baptism with the Holy Spirit, that we rest entirely and absolutely not on anything we do, but upon what Jesus Christ has already done, in dying in our place upon the cross of Calvary (Gal. 3:13; 2 Cor. 5:21).

SECOND STEP

The second step is also in the word "repent," *a change of mind about sin,* a change of mind from that attitude of mind that loves sin or indulges in sin, to that attitude of mind that *renounces sin.* The second step, then, toward the Baptism with the Holy Spirit is to *renounce all sin.* Here again we touch on one of the most vital points in receiving the Baptism with the Holy Spirit. The Holy Spirit is the *Holy* Spirit, and we must make a clean-cut choice between the *Holy* Spirit and *unholy* sin. We cannot have both. It is just at this point that many people fail of the blessing. They read books on the Baptism with the Holy Spirit, they go to conferences and listen to various speakers, they go to "tarrying meetings," they pray long alone for the Baptism with the Holy Spirit, but with no results. Why is it? *Because they are holding on to some sin.*

Men and women oftentimes come to me and say, "I have been praying for the Baptism with the Holy Spirit for a year," or two years, or three years or five years, as the case may be. A missionary came up to me one day in the First Presbyterian Church in New York, at the close of the sermon, and said to me, "I have been praying for the Baptism with the Holy Spirit for twenty years. I have been twenty years a missionary in Persia and I have never had a convert." Think of it! a missionary twenty years and not a convert. Then this minister said, "What is the matter?" When a man comes to me and tells me he has been praying for the Baptism with the Holy Spirit and gets no answer and asks what the trouble is, I generally look him right square in the eye and say, "My brother, it is S-I-N, sin." And to you here this morning who have been praying for a long time for the Baptism with the Holy Spirit and receiving nothing, in all probability the trouble with you is sin; and if I could look down right into your heart right now, just as God is looking right down into your heart at this present moment, I could put my finger on the specific sin that is shutting you out of the blessing. Oftentimes it is what we are pleased to call "a small sin" that shuts us out of the Baptism with the Holy Spirit. In reality there are no small sins. There are sins about small things, but every sin is an act of rebellion against God, no matter how small the thing is in itself and no act of rebellion against God is a small thing. Suppose your little child in a fit of anger throws a book on the floor and you say to the child, "Pick up that book." Now that certainly is a small thing in itself, but suppose the child says, "I won't!" Is it a small thing now? And every sin, no matter how small the thing is in itself, is saying "I won't" to God, and seen in this light, every sin is an appalling thing.

Mr. Finney somewhere tells of a woman in the central part of New York state, who became greatly concerned about the Baptism with the Holy Spirit. When the meetings were over at night, she would go to her room and pray long into the night and lose necessary sleep, and her friends were afraid she would go insane. But there came no answer to her prayers. One night she came home from the meeting and went up to her room. As she knelt there in prayer for the Baptism with the Holy Spirit, some little matter of head adornment came up before her, something that probably would not trouble anybody here, but which was a matter of controversy between her and God, and as she knelt there, she put her hand to her head and took out the pins, threw them across the floor and said, "There! go!" and instantly the Holy Ghost fell upon her. Now, what was it that shut her out of the blessing? Pins? No, controversy with God—sin.

If there is anything that always comes up when you get nearest to God, that is the thing to deal with. You know that with many of us there are things we do and that we have persuaded ourselves are perfectly right, but that every time when we get nearest to God, every time of especial spiritual interest, these things come up to trouble our conscience. Now, if there is anything of that kind that comes up every time you get nearest to God, that is the thing to deal with.

Some years ago I was attending a Bible conference at Dr. Broughton's Tabernacle in Atlanta, Ga. One afternoon when I was to speak on this subject, a minister came in and took a seat over on the right hand side of the tabernacle. As he was taking his seat, Dr. Broughton nudged me and whispered, "Don't look now, or he will think we are talking about him, but that man who is taking his seat is the pope of our denomination in north Georgia. Everything he says goes, but he is not with us at all in this matter. I am glad he is here." As I spoke that afternoon, I would occasionally look over toward that man. He was listening very intently. When the meeting was over and I had gone out into the vestibule of the church, that man was waiting. He came up and said, "I did not stand up this afternoon when you asked people to stand up." I replied, "I noticed you did not." "I thought," he said, "that you said that only those should stand who could say that they were fully surrendered to God." I answered, " That was exactly what I did say." " Well," he answered, " I could not say that." " All right, then you did perfectly right in not getting up. I did not want you to lie." " Say," he continued, " you hit me pretty hard this afternoon." I replied, " That is what I am here for." " You said that if there is any-thing that always came up when we got nearest to God, that was the thing to deal with. Well, there is something that always comes up when I get nearest to God. I am not going to tell you what it is. I think you know." I replied, " I think I do "—I could smell it. " Well," he said, " I just wanted to tell you, that's all." This was on Friday. I left that evening for Augusta, Georgia. The following Tuesday I was coming back through Atlanta on my way to Chicago. The train stopped a few minutes in the station and I got off. Dr. Broughton was waiting in the station to speak to me. He said, " I wish you could have been in our Baptist preachers' meeting yesterday morning. That man from north Georgia came into our meeting and got up and said, ' Brethren, we have been all wrong about this matter,' then he told what he had done [he had put away his sin], then he said, ' Brethren, I have a more definite experience now than I had when I was converted.' " A more definite experience than you had when you were converted is awaiting you this morn-ing, if you will only put away your sin.

THIRD STEP

The third step is also in this verse, " *Be baptized in the name of Jesus Christ unto the remission of your sins.*" THERE MUST BE AN OPEN CONFESSION BEFORE THE WORLD OF OUR RENUNCIATION OF SIN AND OF OUR ACCEPTANCE OF JESUS CHRIST. The Baptism with the Holy Spirit is not for the secret believer, but for the one who comes out openly and confesses before the world his renunciation of sin and acceptance of Jesus Christ. As Mr. Alexander and I went around the world, there were hundreds of people who had been trying to be secret disciples for years who came out and made a public confession of Christ in our meetings and who received blessing through that act.

Of course, God's appointed way of confession of our renunciation of sin and acceptance of Jesus Christ is baptism, and it is in the very act of baptism with water that many receive the Baptism with the Holy Spirit, because that is where they make an open confession of renunciation of sin and acceptance of Jesus Christ. I never felt the importance of baptism before as I did when I was in India. I found that there were in India large numbers of men who really believed the truth about Jesus Christ, who did not hesitate to say that they believed in His Deity and in His atonement, but who would not be baptized. Their reason was that being baptized in India meant great losses to many. For example: A student in the University of Calcutta came to me when I was holding meetings in Calcutta. He said to me, " I believe everything that you have preached." I said, " Why don't you come out, then, and confess Christ in baptism?" He said, " Because if I did, it would cost me everything I have in the world. I am a student of law in the university here in Calcutta. I have not completed my education. My father is a rich man in southern India and I am heir to a fortune; but if I should come out and be baptized, my father would cut me off without an *ana*. There is nothing I could do. I cannot work, for I belong to the Brahmin caste. I cannot practise law, because I have not yet completed my course.

What shall I do?" I replied, "Do what God tells you to do, be baptized in the name of Jesus Christ." After some thought and some reasoning with him, he said, "I will." I was leaving Calcutta, so I could not baptize him, but he went to Dr. Charles Cuthbert Hall, of Brooklyn, New York, who was at that time lecturing in India on the Haskel Foundation, and asked him to baptize him. Dr. Hall consented. The young man sent to his father in southern India, telling him he was to be baptized. His father came up to witness the ceremony and as soon as his son was baptized, he cut him off without an *ana*. I tell you, baptism means something in India. It means something everywhere. If you have not been baptized, either as a child or as an adult, be baptized, make an open confession of your renunciation of sin and of your acceptance of and identification with Jesus Christ in God's appointed way.

But if you have been baptized, even then there should be that for which baptism stands, an open confession of your renunciation of sin and acceptance of and identification with Jesus Christ.

But some one may ask, "Suppose one is a Friend, or, as they are commonly called, a Quaker, who do not believe in the outward sacraments of either the Lord's Supper or baptism? Are they never baptized with the Holy Spirit?" To this I would say that some of those that I have known who gave the clearest evidence of being baptized with the Holy Spirit belonged to the Friends, but I am here to expound the Word of God, and this is what the Word of God says.

The Fourth Step

Now let us turn to Acts 5: 32 and there we will find

the fourth step: "And we are witnesses of these things; and so is the Holy Spirit, Whom God hath given *to them that obey Him.*" THE FOURTH STEP, as set forth in this verse, IS OBEDIENCE. We are told in this verse that God gives the Holy Spirit "*to them that obey Him.*" This step is really found in Acts 2: 38, for, as we saw in studying that verse, we must accept the Lord Jesus, not only as our Saviour, but as our Lord, and that involves obedience, but I have taken you to this verse also, as this verse to some of you will make it more clear.

Let me repeat, the fourth step is obedience. But what is obedience? Some one will say, it is doing what God tells you to do. Yes. But how much that God tells you to do. One thing? two things? three things? No, everything! There is a denomination that greatly emphasizes obedience, as well they might, for it is constantly emphasized throughout the entire Bible; but this particular denomination makes obedience to consist in just one thing, that is, one certain ceremonial act. No, that is not the whole of obedience. *Obedience is not merely doing one, two or three things that God commands, but doing everything that He commands.* The heart of obedience is in the will. *The whole essence of obedience is the surrender of the will to God.* It is coming to God and saying, "Oh God, here I am. Thou hast bought me with a price and I acknowledge Thine ownership. *Send me where Thou wilt, do with me what Thou wilt, use me as Thou wilt.*" THIS IS ONE OF THE MOST FUNDAMENTAL THINGS IN RECEIVING THE BAPTISM WITH THE HOLY SPIRIT, THE UNCONDITIONAL SURRENDER OF THE WILL TO GOD.

More people miss the Baptism with the Holy Spirit at this point, and more people enter experimentally into the Baptism with the Holy Spirit at this point than at almost any other. There are many who go a long ways in the matter of sacrificing for Christ, they even go so far as to go as foreign missionaries and leave home and friends and all the comforts of their own land, to go through sacrifice and suffering on the foreign field, who still stop short of full surrender to God and so stop short of the blessing. Man after man and woman after woman told me in India, men and women who had gone so far as to go to the danger and discomfort of that trying climate, men and women who had given up home and friends and comforts of countless kinds and pretty much everything that most of us hold dear, to go as foreign missionaries, but nevertheless they had not made a full surrender to God as yet. Thank God many of them did then, and therefore were then and there baptized with the Holy Spirit. There is absolutely no use of your praying for the Baptism with the Holy Spirit, nor of going to " tarrying meetings," nor any other kind of meetings, if you will not surrender your will to God, holding absolutely nothing back. You will not receive the Baptism with the Holy Spirit though you pray for it to the crack of doom unless you make an absolute surrender of your will to God.

Many are afraid to make a full surrender to God. They fear that if they should make a full surrender to God, that God would require of them some hard thing, or even some absurd thing. Who is your God, anyway? He certainly is not the God of the Bible. The name of God in the Bible is love, " God is love ;" and absolute surrender to God is simply absolute surrender to infinite love. Is there anything to be dreaded in that? And God's love is not only wiser than that of any earthly father, but more tender than that of any earthly mother.

Some years ago, at one of the Northfield conferences, a gentleman came to me and said, " You must speak on the subject of full surrender. A good many of the men and women over at East Hall (one of the school buildings at which many attendants at the conference were stopping) are greatly troubled on the subject of full surrender. They are afraid that if they make a full surrender to God, that God will require some hard thing of them, or even some absurd thing. The women are afraid that if they tell God they will make a full surrender to Him, He will take away their husbands or do some other dreadful thing, and the men are afraid of some other things." That afternoon I took up the subject of full surrender and repeated what this man had said. Then I said to them, " Who is your God, anyway, that you are afraid to make a full surrender to Him? He certainly is not the God of the Bible, for the name of the God of the Bible is LOVE. Absolute surrender to God is simply putting yourself into the hands of Infinite Love. God's love is not only wiser than that of any earthly father, but more tender than any earthly mother."

Then I used this illustration: " Suppose when I get back to Chicago, my son (who was then perhaps ten years of age), as soon as he hears my ring at the front doorbell, should come running down-stairs and open the door and throw himself into my arms and say, ' Father, I am so glad you are back. We have so greatly missed you since you were away. I want to make this a red-letter day to celebrate your homecoming. I am not going to have any will of my own at all today; I am going to do just what you tell me to do at every turn. Please sit down, Father, and make me out a program for the whole day, telling me just what to do at every hour of the day.'

Now," I said, "suppose my son said that to me, what do you think I would do? Do you think I would call for my wife to bring me a sheet of paper and then sit down and say, 'Clara, what are the things that Reuben most dislikes to do?' and then make him out a program for the day, putting in all the things he most disliked to do? Don't you know that I would not do that? Don't you know that I would make that the brightest, happiest day that Reuben A. Torrey, Jr., ever knew in all his life?" And just so it is with God. When we make an absolute surrender of our wills and all we have to Him, He brings into play all the resources of infinite wisdom and grace and power, to fill our lives with sunshine. He may ask of us things that we would not of ourselves have chosen to do, but if He does, those things will be the very happiest things that we have to do. For years I held back from full surrender to God, indeed from becoming a Christian at all, because I was afraid that God would command me to preach the Gospel; and I was determined to be a lawyer. And God did tell me to preach the Gospel. But today I would rather preach the Gospel than do anything else I know. And so, if any of you are holding back, make a full surrender of your will to God and God will bring into play all the resources of infinite wisdom and love and power to fill your lives with sunshine.

However that may be, *you will not receive the Baptism with the Holy Spirit until you do thus make a full surrender to God,* until you come to Him and say from the depths of your heart and really mean it, " Heavenly Father, here I am. I am Thy property. Thou hast bought me with a price and I acknowledge Thine ownership. Send me where Thou wilt, do with me what Thou wilt, use me as Thou wilt." Through not doing this, thousands today are missing the Baptism with the Holy Spirit and through doing it, thousands upon thousands have entered into blessing.

Some years ago I was attending a Bible Conference at Grove City, Pa. One day a Presbyterian minister came to me and asked if he might have a private conversation with me. I made an appointment with him, and at the time appointed we met. This man was one of the leading Presbyterian ministers in all that part of the state, a man greatly honoured and beloved. When we met, he told me this experience; he said, " Some time ago three young men from my church went to one of the Student Conferences at Northfield. They heard you speak on The Baptism with the Holy Spirit. When they came back, they called upon me in my study and said, ' Pastor, we think we have heard of something at Northfield about which you do not know.' " It seemed to me that that was a rather presumptuous thing for young men in their position to do with a pastor in his position. But notice the quality of the man. He said to them, " Young men, if you have something that I have not, and I ought to have, I want to know about it." Then they told him what they heard at Northfield about the Baptism with the Holy Spirit. " Then," he continued, " when they had gone, I took my hat and walked out into the woods and sat down on a log and looked up to God and said, ' Oh God, if these young men have something that I have not and that I ought to have, I want it right now, and the best I know, I make a full surrender of all I am and all I have to Thee.' Immediately," he continued, " there came stealing into my heart such a sense of peace and joy as I had never known before." Oh, a filling with the Holy Spirit brings to you not only a peace and joy you never knew before, but a power in God's service such as you scarcely dreamed was possible, is awaiting the moment when you make a full, unreserved, unconditional, whole-hearted surrender of all you have and all you are to God.

Many years ago I was speaking in the city of Washington, D. C., at an International Convention of Christian Workers on the Baptism with the Holy Spirit. God was wonderfully present that night. As I closed my address and we joined in prayer, the Holy Spirit manifested His presence in a wonderful way. As I came down from the pulpit, the Chaplain of the United States Senate came to me and said, "I never experienced anything like this before. It seemed to me that if I had opened my eyes, I could have fairly seen the Holy Spirit in this place to-night." But, while many had really entered into the blessing, some had not; and we were there dealing with inquirers for about two hours. About eleven o'clock some one came to me and said, "Do you see that young woman over on the right, with whom Miss Bertha Wright, of Ottawa, Canada, is dealing? Well, she is in great agony. Miss Wright has been dealing with her for two hours. Won't you go over and speak to her?" I went over and stepped into the pew just back of her and leaned over and said, "What is your trouble?" She replied, "I came from Baltimore for just one purpose, and that was that I might be baptized with the Holy Spirit, and I cannot go back to Baltimore until I am." "Is your will fully surrendered to God?" "I do not think it really is." "Well," I said, "it will do no good to pray unless your will is fully surrendered to God. Will you just surrender your will right now?" She replied, "I cannot." "Are you willing that God should lay your will down for you?" "Yes," she replied. "Then," I said, "ask Him to do it."

She bowed her head on the back of the pew in front of her and said, "Oh God, empty me of my self-will. Bring my will into full surrender to Thine. Lay my will down for me. I ask it in Jesus' name." Then I said, "Is it done?" She said, "Yes, it must be. I have asked God for something according to His will and I know He has heard me and I have what I have asked (1 Jno. 5: 14, 15). Yes, it is done, my will is laid down." Then I said, "Now ask Him for the Baptism with the Holy Spirit." Again she bowed her head on the back of the seat in front of her and prayed, "Oh God, baptize me with the Holy Spirit right now. I ask it in Jesus' name," and instantly it was done, *when her will was laid down.*

God is waiting this very moment to baptize any of you who never were baptized with the Holy Spirit before and to fill some of you anew that have been baptized with the Holy Spirit before, the moment that you will lay your will down and then look to Him to baptize or fill you with the Holy Spirit. Go to your rooms, get alone with God somewhere and do it at once.

VIII

THE BAPTISM WITH THE HOLY SPIRIT: HOW TO OBTAIN IT RIGHT NOW

WE saw yesterday that there was a plain path consisting of seven simple steps that any one could take, and that it was absolutely certain that any one who took those steps would enter into the blessing. Yesterday we took up the first four steps. The first step was, to rest upon the finished work of Christ as the sole ground of our acceptance before God. The second step was that we renounce all sin and put every known sin out of our lives. The third step was, an open confession before the world of our renunciation of sin and of our acceptance of Jesus Christ. The fourth step was, absolute surrender to God, that we come to God and say to Him from our hearts, " Heavenly Father, here I am, Thou hast bought me with a price, I acknowledge Thine ownership, now send me where Thou wilt, do with me what Thou wilt, use me as Thou wilt." At this point we closed yesterday.

I. THE FIFTH STEP

You will find the fifth step in John 7: 37-39: " Now on the last day, the great day of the feast, Jesus stood and cried, saying, If any man *thirst*, let him come unto me and drink. He that believeth on me, as the Scripture has said, out of his body shall flow rivers of living water.

But this spake He of the Spirit, which *thev that believe
on Him* were to receive."

Here again we have the first step upon which we dwelt
yesterday, namely, faith in Jesus Christ, "He that believeth on me." But we have also a fifth step in the
word "thirst," "if any man *thirst*." Our Lord Jesus
doubtless had in mind when He uttered these words
Isaiah 44: 3, "For I will pour water *upon him that is
thirsty,* and floods upon the dry ground: *I will pour my
Spirit* upon thy seed, and my blessing upon thine off-
spring." Note carefully the words "*upon him that is
THIRSTY." The fifth step, then, is thirst.* Do you know
what it means to be thirsty, were you ever real thirsty?
I have been, when I was with the troops at Chickamauga
Park during the Spanish-American War. where 60,000
soldiers were gathered together and where there was no
rain for many days, and the air was full of dust thirty
feet high day and night, and we ate dust and drank dust
and slept dust and dreamt dust, and no water fit to drink;
I surely knew what it meant to be thirsty. Again, when
I was in Southern China in 1902, the cholera was raging
and one needed to exercise the utmost care in regard to
what water he drank, I knew what it meant to be thirsty
then. When a man really thirsts, it seems as if every
pore in his body had just one cry, "Water, water, water."
Now apply this to the matter in hand. When a man
thirsts spiritually, his whole being has just one cry, "The
Holy Spirit, the Holy Spirit, the Holy Spirit, O God,
give me the Holy Spirit."

Just as long as we think we can get on some way without the definite Baptism with the Holy Spirit we are not
going to have it. Just as long as we are seeking to accomplish by new tricks of oratory, or by a skillful use of

words, or by all sorts of psychological and other trick methods to influence people, we are not going to have the Baptism with the Holy Spirit; but when we come to the place that we realize our utter need of the Baptism with the Holy Spirit if we are to do effective service for God, and long for it at any cost, then it will be ours, *and not till then.*

Let me illustrate what I mean by two ministers. The first one heard me speaking at the State Convention of the Y. M. C. A. of New York State, at Jamestown, N. Y. I spoke upon this same subject upon which I am speaking to you today, and said very many of the same things I am saying now and said yesterday. This minister, coming out of the hall with another minister, said to him, "That kind of teaching (that is, the kind I have just been giving you) leads either to fanaticism or to despair." He did not ask whether it was scriptural or not. He could not deny that it was scriptural, and he was condemned by it, and tried to escape the condemnation of his own conscience by this smart remark. Now such a man as that is not going to receive the Baptism with the Holy Spirit.

But take another minister. This was at Northfield at one of Mr. Moody's conferences. I had spoken on Saturday night on "The Baptism with the Holy Spirit; What It Is and What It Does, Its Necessity, and Who Can Have It." I was to speak on that Sunday morning on "The Baptism with the Holy Spirit, How to Get It." Early in the morning, this minister came around to the house where I was stopping, and said, "Mr. Torrey, I have come from —— (naming a city in New Jersey where he was pastor) to Northfield for just one purpose, the purpose of being baptized with the Holy Spirit, and

I would rather die than go back to my church without it."
I said to him, "My brother, you are going to have it."
The following Monday morning he had to leave by an
early train, but he came around to see me before he went,
and said, "I want to tell you I have received the Baptism
with the Holy Spirit."

Do you thirst? Do you long for the Baptism with the
Holy Spirit whatever it may involve and whatever it may
cost? It may cost you a good deal. It may take you out
of a nice, comfortable place here in America to China or
to India or the heart of Africa.

Some years ago I was at the International Christian
Workers' Conference at Hartford, Conn. At the close
of one of my addresses on this subject, the pastor and
assistant pastor of the church came to me and asked me
to pray with them that the visitor for the church might
be baptized with the Holy Spirit; and, when the crowd
had gone we knelt together and prayed that she might
be thus baptized. A year later one of the pastors said to
me, "I hardly know whether we would have asked you
to pray that our church visitor might be baptized with the
Holy Spirit, if we had known what it meant, for we have
lost her. She has gone as a foreign missionary," and it
may take some of you from a place of ease and comfort
to a place of hardship and sacrifice, if you really are baptized with the Holy Spirit. Do you want the Holy Spirit
at any cost? If you do not, there is no good whatever in
your praying that you may be filled with the Holy Spirit,
nothing will come of your prayer.

Before I leave this part of the subject let me say that
the desire for the Baptism with the Holy Spirit must be
a pure one. You must desire the Baptism with the Holy
Spirit for the glory of God and not for your own glory.

You must desire the Baptism with the Holy Spirit in order that you may honour God with more effective service and not merely that you may get a new power or a new influence, or it may be a larger salary.

One of the most solemn passages in the Bible on this whole subject brings this out in a very solemn way. You will find it in Acts 8:20-22, " Peter said unto him, thy money perish with thee because thou hast thought that the gift of God may be obtained with money. Thou hast neither part nor lot in this matter: for thy heart is not right in the sight of God. Repent therefore of this thy wickedness, and pray God if perhaps the thought of thine heart may be forgiven thee." Simon, the magician, had seen the power that Peter and John had because they had been baptized with the Holy Spirit, and he desired a similar power for himself. He was willing to pay large money for it and offered it, but his unholy desire, intense though it was, only brought denunciation and not a blessing on his head. Be very careful at this point. Get alone with God and ask God to search you and show you whether your desire for this wonderful blessing is a pure desire, in order that you may glorify God as you ought, or a selfish, unholy desire, simply in order that you may get greater joy or greater power for yourself.

II. THE SIXTH STEP

You will find the sixth step in a very familiar passage of Scripture, Luke 11:13, " If ye then, being evil, know how to give good gifts unto your children: how much more shall your heavenly Father give the Holy Spirit *to them that ask Him*." THAT IS THE SIXTH STEP, JUST ASK HIM. That is, ask God definitely for the definite

Baptism with the Holy Spirit. THE SIXTH STEP IS DEFINITE PRAYER FOR THIS DEFINITE BLESSING. There are many in these days, and they are often well known men, excellent men, too, who tell us that we ought not to pray for the Holy Spirit, and they reason it out very speciously. They say "the Holy Spirit was given to the Church as an abiding possession at Pentecost" (that is true), and then they ask "why pray for what you have already got?" To this the late Dr. A. J. Gordon replied conclusively, "Jesus Christ was given to the world as an abiding gift at Calvary (which is certainly true, see John 3:16), He was given to the world as a whole, but each individual in the world must appropriate this gift for himself. Just so the gift of the Holy Spirit was given to the whole Church at Pentecost, but it was given to the Church as a whole, and each individual member of the Church must appropriate the gift for himself, and God's way of appropriation is prayer."

But these brethren often go still further, and they say "every individual believer in Christ has the Holy Spirit," and that is true also, as we saw a few days ago. We are told definitely in Romans 8:9, "If any man have not the Spirit of Christ (and "the Spirit of Christ" here does not mean a Christlike spirit as it is so often misinterpreted, but is a name of the Holy Spirit), he is none of His;" so it is clear that every believer has the Holy Spirit in some sense. And these brethren go on and say if then every believer already has the Holy Spirit why pray for Him? To which the all-sufficient answer is, that it is one thing to have the Holy Spirit dwelling in us (as He does in every believer) way back in some hidden corner of our being where we are not distinctly conscious of His presence, and quite another thing and a far more glorious thing to have this indwelling Spirit take entire possession of the house that He inhabits, as He does when one is baptized (or, filled) with the Holy Spirit.

Anyway, against all these specious reasonings of men we put the plain, unquestionable utterance of Jesus Christ, Luke 11:13, "If ye then, being evil, know how to give good gifts unto your children: how much more shall your heavenly Father give the Holy Spirit *to them that ask Him.*"

Some years ago I was on a program of the International Christian Workers' Convention at Boston, to speak on the subject of the Baptism with the Holy Spirit, on the last evening of the convention. One of the men came to me at the noon hour (a most excellent brother) and he said, "I notice you are on the program this evening to speak on the Baptism with the Holy Spirit." I said, "Yes." Then he said, "I think that is the most important subject on the program." I replied, "I think it is important." "Be sure to tell them," he continued, "not to pray for the Holy Spirit." "My brother," I replied, "I will tell them to do the very thing that you tell me to tell them not to do; *for God has said,* ' how much more shall your heavenly Father give the Holy Spirit to *them that ask Him.*'" "Oh, yes," he said, "but that was before Pentecost." "All right," I said, "how about Acts 4:31, was that before Pentecost or after?" He replied, "It was certainly after." "Well," I said, "take it and read it—And *when they had prayed* the place was shaken where they were assembled together; *and they were all filled with the Holy Ghost,* and they spoke the word of God with boldness." "How about Acts 8:15, 16, was that before or after Pentecost?" "Well," he said, "it was certainly after Pentecost." I said, "Take it and read it." He read, " Peter and John when they were come down, *prayed* for them, *that they might receive the Holy Ghost:* (for as yet He was fallen upon none of them: only they were baptized unto the name of the Lord Jesus)." So you may go right through your Bible, and after Pentecost as well as before Pentecost you will find both by explicit statement and by illustrative example that men and women were " baptized," or were " filled with the Holy Spirit," *when they prayed.*

But with me this is not a mere matter of mere exegesis. If it were, I would believe it whether I had experience or not, for when I find a thing written in the Bible I believe it, experience or no experience, for I do not believe in trying to bring the Bible down to the level of our experience but in bringing our experience up to the level of the Bible. But with me this is a matter of definite and absolutely certain experience. I know that God baptizes men with the Holy Spirit as they pray, and that He fills those that have been baptized with the Holy Spirit anew with the Holy Spirit as they pray, just as definitely as I know that water quenches thirst and that food satisfies hunger. I know it from my own personal experience. How often as I have prayed alone, or as I have prayed in the company of like-minded believers, the Holy Spirit has fallen upon us just as definitely and consciously as I have heard the rain falling on the roof of a building or felt it pouring down over my whole body.

Let me give you one illustration. Some years ago the ministers of Chicago were holding daily noon prayer-meetings in the Y. M. C. A. building in Chicago as a preparation for an expected visit of Mr. Moody to that city. It was my privilege to preside at those prayer-meetings. One noon in the midst of the meeting a

Baptist minister sprang to his feet and said, "Brother Torrey, what we need here in Chicago is an all-night prayer-meeting of the ministers." "Very well," I replied, "if the ministers of Chicago desire an all-night prayermeeting, if they will come up to the Chicago Avenue Church (the Moody Church) next Friday night at ten o'clock, we will have a prayer-meeting and if God keeps us there all night we will stay all night, we will stay as long as God keeps us." That night at ten o'clock, perhaps six or seven hundred gathered in the prayer-meeting room of the Chicago Avenue Church. They were not all ministers. There were many other Christian workers, as well as some Christian women.

Were you ever in a meeting where the devil made a dead set to spoil the meeting? Well, that was the kind of a meeting that we had at first. For example, three men got down near the door at the far end of the room by three chairs and commenced to pound and shout and shriek in a pretense of prayer, and when someone expostulated with them, saying that things should "be done decently and in order," they swore at the man who expostulated with them. A little later a man sprang to his feet over at my left and proclaimed that he was Elijah. The man was not to blame, he was a lunatic. There were seven of whom I knew in the United States at that time who claimed to be Elijah, and he was one of the seven. Some of the more timid ones began to think, "Well, if this is the kind of a meeting it is going to be, I am going home." But the great bulk of us were there for a blessing and we were determined to stay until we got it.

About midnight God gave us complete victory. All the discordant elements were eliminated; and oh! what praying there was from that time on up to a little after two in the morning. I think I had never heard such praying before and have seldom heard such praying since. At 2:15 (I know the time, for I had taken out my watch a few moments before), we were all on our knees, and suddenly the Holy Spirit fell upon us. No one could speak, no one could pray, no one could sing. All you could hear was the subdued sobbing of joy unspeakable and full of glory. It seemed to me as I knelt there that if I had looked up I would fairly have seen the Holy Spirit in that place. This was early Saturday morning. The following morning, Sunday morning, at the close of my morning service, one of my deacons came to me, he could hardly speak yet, and grasped my hand and whispered, " Brother Torrey, I will never forget yesterday morning to the latest day of my life."

But it was not all mere emotion, no, thank God, no. Men went out from that meeting in the early morning hours to different places with the power of God resting upon them. One business man went down to Missouri on an early morning train. After he had transacted his business he asked the proprietor of the hotel if there was any meeting going on in that town. He replied, " Yes, Brother W——, there is a protracted meeting going on up at the Cumberland Presbyterian Church." The man was a Cumberland Presbyterian himself, and he went up to the church. After the meeting was opened, he arose in his seat, he was a well known man in his denomination, and asked the minister if he could say a few words. The minister replied, " Certainly, Brother W——." That man poured out his soul, and a little after I heard that there were fifty-eight people converted while he was speaking. Another young man, Emil Lindfield, who afterwards died as a very successful missionary in South Africa, went in the early morning hours to Baraboo, Wisconsin, and I soon heard from Baraboo that there had been thirty-eight young men and boys converted while he spoke. And a little while later, I received a letter from a Methodist minister in Wisconsin, near Milwaukee, asking me if we had a young man named Samuel J—— in our Institute. He said that a young man had appeared in their midst, a perfect stranger, and said that he was Samuel J——, of the Bible Institute of Chicago, that he had been speaking in the schoolhouses, Methodist Church and Soldiers' Home and that there were conversions wherever he spoke. This man also had gone out early that morning and up to that section with the Spirit of God resting upon him.

As I went around the world, in 1902 and the years that followed, in pretty much every field that I visited, Japan, China, New Zealand, Australia, England, Scotland and Ireland, and other lands, I met with men or women who had gone out from that meeting with the power of God resting upon them. Yes, and we today can go out from this meeting to the uttermost parts of the earth, with the power of God resting upon us, to accomplish mighty things for Him. Yes, beyond the possibility of honest question, God does baptize men and women with the Holy Spirit, and fill anew with the Holy Spirit those who have already been thus baptized, AS THEY PRAY.

II. The Seventh Step

We have now come to the seventh and last step, in some respects the simplest of all and yet to many the most difficult of all, and also the place where more people miss the blessing than almost anywhere else. You will find this step set forth in the words of Christ in Mark 11:24: "Therefore I say unto you, what things soever ye desire, when ye pray, *believe that ye receive them,* and *ye shall have them." The seventh step is faith. Simply expecting from God what you ask,* THE BAPTISM WITH THE HOLY SPIRIT. No matter how definite any promise of God's Word may be, we never realize it in our own experience until we believe it. For example, we are told in James 1:5, "If any of you lacketh wisdom, let him ask of God, that giveth to all men liberally and upbraideth not; and *it shall be given him."* Now that is certainly unqualifiedly positive, nothing could possibly be more positive. But James did not stop there, he went on to say, "*But let him ask in faith,* nothing doubting: for he that doubteth is like the surge of the sea driven by the wind and tossed. For let not that man think that he shall receive anything of the Lord." Just so it is in this matter, God's promise is definite enough, *but unless we believe the promise* and *confidently expect God to do what He has so definitely promised to do,* our prayer will bring no result. Here is where a countless multitude of earnest seekers for the Baptism with the Holy Spirit fail of obtaining the blessing, they do not confidently expect. They meet the other conditions, they pray definitely and earnestly, but they do not confidently expect and therefore they do not get.

But *there is a faith that goes beyond expectation. There is a faith that puts out its hand and takes on the spot the very thing it asks of God.* That comes out in the Revised Version of Mark 11:24: "Therefore I say unto you, all things whatsoever ye pray and ask for, *believe* that ye *have received them,* and ye shall have them." (The American Standard Revision has gone back to the translation of the Authorized Version, "believe that ye receive them," but without warrant in the Greek text. Indeed, they say themselves in the margin, ' Greek, *received,*' well if that is the Greek why do they not put it into the text, for we ought to know *exactly what Jesus Christ said*). This change in the Revised Version greatly bothered me when it first appeared. I got one of the earliest copies of the Revised New Testament. You will remember that the New Testament came out before the Old did, and I secured one of the very earliest copies. I started in at the first chapter of Matthew, at the first verse, and noted every change in the Revised Version from "the Authorized Version," and compared them both with the best Greek text, and noted every change in the margin of my own Bible with my own hand. I do not need to do that any longer; for the Oxford Publishing Company has published a Bible, the Two Version Bible, in which the changes are indicated in the margin. I got on very nicely for the most part, and saw in how many instances the Revised Version was from a better Greek text than "the Authorized Version," or a more accurate translation, or a more modern rendering of the words and therefore in more easily understandable English. But one day I came to Mark 11:24, and I read the Authorized Version, "What things soever ye desire when ye pray, believe that ye receive them and ye shall have them." That was plain enough; then I turned to the Revised Version and read, "All things whatsoever ye pray and ask for believe *that ye have received them* and ye shall have them." I said to myself, what nonsense, what a confusion of the tenses, "believe that ye *have received* them," past tense. "and ye shall have them," future tense, in other words, " believe that you have received " and " *you shall have what you have already got.*"

Then I turned to the Greek text, and I found out that whether it was sense or nonsense, the Revised Version was the right rendering of the Greek text, only it should have used the aorist instead of the perfect tense. " Well," I said, " it must be so, but what does it mean," and for the life of me I could not tell and I did not discover for years. But some years later I said to my people in Minneapolis, " I am going to take you through the First Epistle of John, verse by verse. I will study the verses during the week and will give to you on the Lord's Day what I find during the week, and if I find anything in First John that does not agree with my theology, I will change my theology at that point." Well, I got on very nicely until I got to the last chapter, although I did have to change my theology at some points. One day in my study, I came to 1 John 5: 14, 15, " And this is the confidence that we have toward Him, that, if we ask anything according to His will, He heareth us: and if we know that He heareth us whatsoever we ask, *we know that we have* the petitions which we have asked of Him." And then I understood Mark 11: 24. Do you see it?

I see that some of you do and some of you do not. Well, I will explain it so that every child here can understand it. When you come to God in prayer, the first question to ask is, " Is that petition that I asked of God *according to His will'?*" If it is definitely promised in His Word, then, of course, you know it is "according to His will." Now then read 1 John 5: 14, " And this is the confidence that we have toward Him, that, if we ask anything according to His will, He heareth us." Then saying to yourself, " I asked this definite thing, I know

it is according to God's will because it is definitely promised in His Word, therefore according to 1 John 5 : 14 I
know that He has heard me." Then read the fifteenth
verse, " And if we know that He heareth us whatsoever
we ask, *we know that we have the petitions* which we
have asked of Him," and claim the thing as yours, not
because you feel it but because God so definitely says so
in His Word.

Now apply this to the matter of the Baptism with the
Holy Spirit. You have taken all the other six steps, and
you have come to God and asked Him definitely to baptize you with the Holy Spirit (or, to fill you with the
Holy Spirit, as the case may be). Then ask yourself, " Is
this petition of mine according to His will? " You know
that it is because Acts 2 : 39 and Luke 11 : 13 say so.
Then read 1 John 5 : 14, " This is the confidence that we
have toward Him, that, *if we ask anything according to
His will, He heareth us."* Then say, " I asked the Baptism with the Holy Spirit, I know that is according to His
will because God says so in Luke 11 : 13 and Acts 2 : 39,
therefore, I know He has heard me." Then read the fifteenth verse, " and *if we know that He heareth us* whatsoever we ask, *we know that we have the petitions which
we have asked of Him."* The petition I asked was the
Baptism with the Holy Spirit, I know He has heard me,
I know I have what I asked, I KNOW I HAVE THE BAP-
TISM WITH THE HOLY SPIRIT. And WHAT YOU THUS
TAKE UPON NAKED FAITH IN THE WORD OF GOD,
YOU SHALL AFTERWARDS HAVE IN ACTUAL EXPERIMENTAL
POSSESSION.

Let me give you a concrete illustration. Mr. F. B.
Meyer, of London, and I had gone together to a Students'
Conference at Lake Geneva, Wisconsin. He spoke that

night on the Baptism with the Holy Spirit. When he finished he said, "If any of you wish to speak to Mr. Torrey or myself about this matter, we will stay and talk with you after the meeting is over." A young man came to me who had just graduated from the Illinois College. He said, "I heard of this blessing a month ago and I have been praying for it ever since but I do not get it, what is the matter?" I said, "Is your will laid down, is your will fully surrendered to God?" He replied, "No, I don't think it is." I said, "Well, your praying will do no good until your will is laid down. Will you lay your will down now?" He said, "I cannot." Then I said, "Are you willing that God should lay it down for you?" He said, "I am." Then I said, "Let us kneel down and ask God to do it." I put two chairs side by side, and we knelt down by them. I opened my Bible to 1 John 5 : 14. 15 and laid it open on the chair in front of the young man. "Now," I said, "ask God to lay your will down for you." He prayed, "Heavenly Father, lay my will down for me, empty me of my self-will, bring my will into absolute surrender to Thine own, I ask it in the name of the Lord Jesus." I said, "Is it done?" He said, "It must be, I have asked something according to His will and I know He has heard me and I know He has done what I ask of Him." I said, "All right. What is it you want?" He replied, "I want the Baptism with the Holy Spirit." I said, "Ask for it." Again he prayed, "Heavenly Father, baptize me with the Holy Spirit righ', now. I ask it in the name of the Lord Jesus." I asked, "Is it done?" He said, "I don't feel it." I said, "That is not what I asked you. Read again the verse before you," and he read, "This is the confidence we have in Him, that, if we ask anything according to His will, He heareth us." I said, "Was what you asked something according to His will?" He said, "It was, Luke 11 : 13 and Acts 2 : 39 say so." Then I said, "What, then, do you know?" He said, "I know He hears me." "All right, read the next verse," and he read, "And if we know He heareth us whatsoever we ask, we know that we have the petitions that we have asked of Him." I said, "What do you know?" He said, "I know that I have the petition that I have asked of Him." I said, "What is the petition that you asked of Him?" He said, "The Baptism with the Holy Spirit." I said, "What do you know?" He replied, "*I know that I have the Baptism with the Holy Spirit;* I don't feel it, but God says so." We got up; I had a few more words with him and he went to his tent and I went to mine.

The next morning I took the boat for an early train to Chicago. I came back a few days later; I saw this young man down in the audience, and standing on the platform I looked over to him where he was sitting in the amphitheatre and said, "Did you really receive the Baptism with the Holy Spirit?" He did not need to answer, for his face told the story. But he did answer, that he had. Two or three years later I told this incident at a meeting of the Methodist ministers in Chicago, and an inquisitive brother asked me, "Well, what became of the young man?" I had to reply, "I do not know." But within two weeks, as I was sitting in my office in the Bible Institute of Chicago, there came a rap at my door. I said, "Come in." A fine-looking young fellow walked in. He said, "Do you recognize me?" I replied, "I know I have seen you somewhere, but I cannot place you." Well, it was this young man. He was now in the Chicago Theological Seminary. A few days later a group of students from the Chicago Theological Seminary came over to invite me to speak at the seminary on the Day of Prayer for Colleges. I asked them how this young man was getting on, and they told me he was getting on in a wonderful way, that although he was only a middler in the seminary, the seminary had already given him a church up in Wisconsin, which, they added, was a very unusual thing, but they said something better still, " He is having conversions all the time."

When The Day of Prayer came, I went over to the seminary and spoke on the Baptism with the Holy Spirit and the Spirit of God came upon them. After I had left the room they began praying in English, French, Norwegian, Swedish, Danish and German—no supernatural gift of tongues, these were the native languages of the different students—and President Fiske, President of the seminary at that time, wrote to the Boston Congregationalist that they had a perfect Pentecost; and it all came through this young fellow who took the Baptism with the Holy Spirit by naked faith in the simple Word of God, at Lake Geneva, and any one in this auditorium this morning can take it the same way right now.

IV. THREE QUESTIONS

Now there are some very important questions that some of you would like to ask me, so I am going to ask them for you.

1. The first question that some of you will want to ask is, MUST WE KNOW NOT THAT WE HAVE THE BAPTISM WITH THE HOLY SPIRIT BEFORE WE TAKE UP OUR WORK? Yes, we certainly should. BUT HOW KNOW? There are two ways of knowing things: First, by the plain statement of God's Word, and Second, by experience; and

knowing by God's Word is a surer way of knowing than knowing by experience. Our experiences, or at least, our feelings, come and go, according to what we are eating or the state of our health; *but the Word of God always remains the same;* and as we have just seen, *you can know by the naked Word of God* right today *that you have received the* Baptism with the Holy Spirit. Whether you have felt it or not, you can claim it by simple faith in the inerrantly inspired Word of God.

2. But some of you will desire to ask a second question. MAY WE NOT HAVE TO WAIT FOR SOME TIME FOR THE BAPTISM WITH THE HOLY SPIRIT *just as the Apostles had to wait ten days between the day when the Lord Jesus gave the promise and Pentecost?* In answer to this question, I would ask, "Have you never noticed that the Bible tells us just why the disciples had to wait ten days?" Read Acts 2: 1, 2 and you will find out just why the disciples had to wait ten days: "And when the day of Pentecost was *fully come* (the Greek is, '*was being fulfilled*'), they were all with one accord in one place. And suddenly there came a sound from heaven as of the rushing of a mighty wind, and it filled all the house where they were sitting." In other words, the Holy Ghost could not come upon them *until the day of Pentecost had fully come.* Way back in the Old Testament types, yes, way back in the eternal counsels of God, the Day of Pentecost was set for the imparting of the gift of the Holy Spirit and the gathering of the Church; and He could not be given therefore until the Day of Pentecost was fully come. But now the Day of Pentecost has fully come and THERE IS NO NEED OF TARRYING NOW. Was there any waiting after Pentecost? Read Acts 4: 31, "And when they had prayed the

place was shaken wherein they were gathered together; they were *all filled with the Holy Ghost.*"

Was there any waiting in the household of Cornelius? They were listening to the first gospel sermon they had ever heard and Peter reached the climax of his sermon, Acts 10:43, " To Him (that is, to the Lord Jesus) give all the prophets witness, that through His name every one that believeth on Him shall receive remission of sins," and instantly they all believed and immediately the Holy Ghost fell upon them, right then and there. Was there any waiting in the case of Saul of Tarsus? We read in Acts 9:17, " And Ananias departed, and entered into the house (that is, the house where Saul of Tarsus was waiting in his blindness); and laying his hands on him said, Brother Saul, the Lord, even Jesus, who appeared unto thee in the way which thou camest, hath sent me, that thou mayest receive thy sight, *and be filled with the Holy Ghost.*" And he took him and baptized him, then prayed with him, *and immediately he was filled with the Holy Ghost,* baptized with the Holy Ghost; and we read two verses farther down, " And *straightway* in the synagogues he proclaimed Jesus, that He is the Son of God. And all that heard him were amazed and said, is not this he that in Jerusalem made havoc of them which called on this name? . . . But Saul, increased the more in strength, *and confounded the Jews which dwelt at Damascus, proving that this is the Christ.*"

They did have to wait at Ephesus, but simply because the fault was entirely in themselves, they did not know that the Holy Spirit was yet given; but when Paul told them He had been given and they took the necessary steps, they were all baptized with the Holy Ghost right then and there, before the meeting broke up. So you may have to wait, but if so, the reason of waiting will not be in God but in yourself. It is the will of God that every child of His who has not already been baptized with the Holy Spirit should be so baptized today, but you may delay the blessing by not resting upon the finished work of Christ as the sole ground of your acceptance before God, or by not putting away every known sin, or by not openly confessing your renunciation of sin and your acceptance of Christ before the world, or by not making a full surrender to God, or by not desiring the blessing at any cost, or by not definitely praying, or by not expecting and claiming it right here now. But if you do have to wait ten days or even ten minutes, the trouble will be entirely with you and not with God. ANY ONE OF YOU MAY BE BAPTIZED WITH THE HOLY SPIRIT BEFORE YOU LEAVE THIS BUILDING, or if you have already been thus baptized, be filled anew.

3. But there is a third question that some of you will wish to ask, and it is a very important one, and that is this: WILL THERE BE NO MANIFESTATION OF THE BAPTISM WITH THE HOLY SPIRIT WHEN WE ARE THUS BAPTIZED, AND WILL EVERYTHING BE JUST THE SAME AS IT WAS BEFORE, AND IF IT IS, WHAT IS THE GOOD OF IT ANYWAY? Yes, indeed, there will be a manifestation; but please notice two things: First, the character of the manifestation; Second, the time of the manifestation.

First, let us take up *The Character of the Manifestation,* or, *How the Baptism with the Holy Spirit Will Manifest Itself in Your Case.* Some of you possibly expect the manifestation to be " the gift of tongues," or " speaking in tongues," and expect no other; but, as we saw the other day, such expectation is entirely unscriptural and such dictation to the Holy Spirit is contrary to the plain teaching of the Word of God. But some of you will expect an entirely different manifestation. Very likely you have read the story of the experience of John Wesley, and Charles G. Finney, and D. L. Moody. All of these tell very nearly the same story. Mr. Finney put it about this way, that when he was baptized with the Holy Ghost, great waves like electricity swept over him, and he had to pray to God to withhold his hand lest he die from very ecstasy on the spot. Mr. Moody, though he seldom told it, had a somewhat similar experience. Now many of you expect something like that. I do not deny the reality of these experiences. The word of men like Charles G. Finney and D. L. Moody is to be believed; and there is another reason why I do not deny them, which I probably would better not mention. But I challenge any one to show me anywhere in the Bible one single record of any such an experience. I am inclined to think that the apostles had them; but if they did they kept them to themselves, and I am glad they did, for if any one of them had described such an experience that is what we would all have been looking for.

What was the manifestation in every case recorded in the Bible? SOME NEW POWER IN SERVICE. On the Day of Pentecost, they spoke with the tongues of the different people who were there present, spoke " the mighty works of God " in those tongues (Acts 2: 6, 8, 11). They were understood by the people there present, resulting in a great number of definite conversions of people who heard them speaking in the tongues in which they were born. The " speaking with other tongues " on this occasion had not the slightest resemblance to the " speaking with tongues " of which some boast today.

In the case of Saul of Tarsus, there was no record of

his speaking in tongues at that time, although we have reason to know that Paul did at some times alone by himself speak with tongues, but he declared that in the public assembly, " I had rather speak five words *with my understanding,* that *by my voice I might teach others also,* than ten thousand words in a tongue " (1 Cor. 14:19). What was the manifestation in Paul's case? Turn to Acts 9:17-22, and you will find the manifestation was simply this, that *he proclaimed Jesus as the Christ with irresistible power;* and THAT WILL BE THE ESSENTIAL CHARACTER OF THE MANIFESTATION IN YOUR CASE, NEW POWER IN THE WORK THAT GOD HAS CALLED YOU TO DO.

Now let us look at THE TIME OF THE MANIFESTATION. *When will the manifestation come?* AFTER WE TAKE THE BAPTISM WITH THE SPIRIT ON SIMPLE FAITH IN THE NAKED WORD OF GOD. God's order is this: First, God's Word, God's promise; Second, our faith in the Word of God, simply because God says it; Third—experience. The human heart tries to change God's order and have First, the Word, the promise of God; Second, experience; and then Third, faith. But that is not faith at all. Take the case of Abraham. God told Abraham that he was to be a father of many nations. Abraham had no reason for believing it other than the Word of God. In itself it was incredible; he was 100 years old and his wife nearly that. They were both beyond the age of having children, but the record is that " Abraham *believed God,*" and " God reckoned " Abraham's simple faith in the unsupported Word of God (just because God said it) " for righteousness." Abraham had no thrills then! No, just God's Word, that and that alone. He had thrills enough when the child was born, and he saw Isaac with his own eyes, *because he believed God's naked Word*. THE ONE THING THAT GOD DEMANDS OF MEN IS THAT MEN BE- LIEVE WHAT HE SAYS JUST BECAUSE HE SAYS IT; that's faith. Whenever you require some feeling or some ex- perience before you believe God's Word, you are making God a liar.

Take my own experience. I had been a minister for some years before I came to the place where I saw that I had no right to preach until I was definitely baptized with the Holy Ghost. I went to a business friend of mine and said to him in private, "I am never going to enter my pulpit again until I have been baptized with the Holy Spirit and know it, or until God in some way tells me to go." Then, just as far as I could, I shut myself up alone in my study and spent the time continually on my knees asking God to baptize me with the Holy Spirit. As the days passed, the devil tried to tempt me by saying, "Sup- pose Sunday comes and you are not baptized with the Holy Spirit, what then?" I replied, "Whatever comes, I will not go into my pulpit and preach again until I have been baptized with the Holy Spirit and know it, or God in some way tells me to go; even though I have to tell my people that I have never been fit to preach." But Sunday did not come before the blessing came. I had it more or less definitely mapped out in my mind what would happen; but what I had mapped out in my mind did not happen. I recall the exact spot where I was kneeling in prayer in my study. I could go to the very spot in that house at 1348 N. Adams St., Minneapolis. It was a very quiet moment, one of the most quiet mo- ments I ever knew; indeed, I think one reason I had to wait so long was because it took that long before my soul could get quiet before God. Then God simply said to me, not in any audible voice, but in my heart, " It's yours. Now go and preach." Oh, if I had only known my Bible better. He had already said it to me in His Word in 1 John 5: 14, 15; but I did not then know my Bible as well as I know it now, and God had pity on my ignorance and said it directly to my soul. You do not need to have it said directly to your soul; for I have shown it to you this morning in His Word.

I went and preached, and I have been a new minister from that day to this. I was then the pastor of a very small and obscure church, though I had taken two degrees at Yale and had studied at two German universities. But from that time my field began to wonderfully enlarge until at last I had preached the gospel around the world and had seen I suppose hundreds of thousands converted to Christ.

Some time after this experience (I do not recall just how long after), while sitting in my room one day, that very same room, I recall just where I was sitting, before my revolving bookcase, I do not know whether I was thinking about this subject at all, I do not remember, but suddenly, as near as I can describe it, though it does not exactly describe it, I was struck from my chair on to the floor and I found myself shouting (I was not brought up to shout and I am not of a shouting temperament, but I shouted like the loudest shouting Methodist) " glory to God, glory to God, glory to God," and I could not stop. I tried to stop, but it was just as if some other power than my own was moving my jaws. At last, when I had succeeded in pulling myself together, I went down-stairs and told my wife what had happened. But that was not when I was baptized with the Holy Spirit. I was baptized with the Holy Spirit when I took Him by simple

faith in the naked Word of God, and any one of you can
be thus baptized today, yes, you can be thus baptized
before you leave this building this afternoon. God grant
that you may be. What I am trying to get you to do
more than all else is just to get you to believe God's
Word without any other guarantee and to take the Baptism with the Holy Spirit by simple faith in God's Word.

Let me tell you one more incident before I close. July
8, 1894, I was at a Students' Convention at Northfield,
Mass. The preceding night I had spoken in Stone Hall
upon " The Baptism with the Holy Spirit; What It Is,
What It Does, Who Needs It, and Who Can Have It,"
and now the closing Sunday morning service was being
held in the Congregational Church, and I was speaking
on " The Baptism with the Holy Spirit, How To Obtain
It." I said very much what I have said to you this afternoon and yesterday afternoon. As I finished, I took out
my watch and saw that it was exactly twelve o'clock. I
turned to that great body of students and said, " Mr.
Moody has invited us to go up on the mountain this afternoon at three o'clock to pray that we may receive the
Holy Spirit. It is now exactly twelve o'clock, it is three
hours to three o'clock, some of you cannot wait three
hours and you do not need to. Go to your room in the
hotel, go to your room in the buildings, go to your tent,
go out into the woods, go anywhere where you can get
alone with God and have this matter out with God."

That afternoon at three o'clock we all met up in front
of Mr. Moody's mother's house, she was still living then.
Then we went down through the lane and through the
gate, 456 of us in all, Paul Moody counted us as we went
through the gate. Four hundred and fifty-six men from
Yale, Harvard. Amherst. Dartmouth and other Eastern

colleges, and went up the mountain side. After we had gone some distance, Mr. Moody said, "I think we do not need to go any farther, let us stop here." He sat down on a stump, others sat down on logs, or on the ground. Mr. Moody said, "Before we go to God in prayer, have any of you anything to say?" One after another of those men arose, I should think about seventy-five in all (as I recall it), and said in substance, "Mr. Moody, I could not wait until three o'clock, I have been alone with God and I believe I have been baptized with the Holy Spirit." When these testimonies were over, Mr. Moody said, "I can see no reason why we should not kneel down right here now and ask God that the Holy Spirit may come upon us just as definitely as He came upon the Apostles on the Day of Pentecost. Let us pray." We knelt in prayer, some of us lay on the ground on our faces (there were no women present; all men), and we began to pray. As we had gone up the mountain side clouds had been gathering over the mountain, and as we began to pray, the clouds broke and the raindrops began to fall upon us through the overhanging pine needles. But another cloud had been gathering over Northfield for ten days, a cloud big with the grace and power of God. As we began to pray our prayers seemed to pierce that cloud, and the Holy Ghost fell upon us.

Men and women, if I am any judge, a cloud has been gathering over this building for some days, a cloud big with the grace and power of God. Why not pierce that cloud with our prayers right now?